I, ZIPPORAH

MAURINE GEORGIADES

ISBN 978-1-64191-238-9 (paperback)
ISBN 978-1-64191-239-6 (digital)

Copyright © 2018 by Maurine Georgiades

All rights reserved. No part of this publication may be reproduced, distributed, or transmitted in any form or by any means, including photocopying, recording, or other electronic or mechanical methods without the prior written permission of the publisher. For permission requests, solicit the publisher via the address below.

Christian Faith Publishing, Inc.
832 Park Avenue
Meadville, PA 16335
www.christianfaithpublishing.com

Printed in the United States of America

The Stranger

"Ho-ho, my daughters! How did you come so soon today?" Jeh-Jeh asks, his left eyebrow rising in surprise.

We seven sisters tell him, between giggles, about the Egyptian man who was sitting by the well. We explain that we had started to draw water and fill the troughs; but, again, the rude and crude shepherds came and drove us and our sheep away.

I stop giggling long enough to tell Jeh-Jeh how the Egyptian man delivered us from those mean shepherds and filled the water troughs so all of our sheep could drink calmly this evening.

"The Egyptian man—where is he?" asks Jeh-Jeh. "Why did you leave him there? Why didn't you invite him to have bread with us? Zipporah, go back and bring him here. The rest of you need to oversee the slaves and prepare a festive meal." With a wave of his hand he dismisses us.

Why have I been chosen to bring the alien to break bread with us? I dash to the women's quarters for my bag and for my long silk scarf. Without the scarf, how can I enjoy the journey?

Which god is the protector for such an ecstatic evening as I am about to enjoy? I bow briefly to each of the gods as I escape the compound and eagerly head for the well.

Ah, the joy of being free in the breeze! I dance on my toes in the sand, twirling and pirouetting to a mystical tune, the silk scarf swirling gracefully above my head. Shadows dance beside me in sheer delight. For these moments I am the queen of a faraway exotic shore, the evening breeze my escort.

With riotous abandon I whirl and prance as the sun is lowering. I have no fear of any lecherous men in our vast area. Because of Jeh-Jeh they dare not touch me. They prefer to keep heads on their shoulders.

The middle of seven sisters, I'm the muse and mystic, quixotic and mysterious in their eyes whenever they catch glimpses of my wandering fantasies. Jeh-Jeh would understand. He says I'm very like my birth mother. But then he says no more.

Shadows get longer. As I near the well, dancing and fantasy cease. I tuck the silk scarf into my bag and sedately cover head and shoulders with my shawl. The Egyptian man must be greeted by a modestly clad woman.

He sits pensively on the stone. He sees me approach and rises. He is imposingly tall and strongly built. His eyes pierce through the space between us, and I find myself quailing in his presence.

In what language can I deliver Jeh-Jeh's invitation? With uncommon timidity, I stammer, "Prince Jethro, priest of Midian, wants you to come and sup with him." Can he understand?

He nods and answers in a foreign tongue. Somehow, I perceive he will come. He must first bathe. Of course.

I point to the far yonder terebinth tree where I shall wait for him. Again he nods. Do I detect a faint smile as I turn away? Or is it a smirk?

Now under the terebinth tree, I sit beside my mother's grave. Childbirth gave me the breath of life but took her breath away. From my bag I bring out the unusual stone I had found months ago. Gently I lay it on her grave, my tears washing away the dust and exposing a wonder of rare beauty, my gift of love to the mother I never knew.

I wipe away my tears as the Egyptian man strides near, erect even with a large bag over his shoulder, and somehow authoritative in his very movements. I feel intimidated. I rise as gracefully as I'm able, and begin the long walk toward Jeh-Jeh—and to safety.

Who is this man who follows me? A spy? Someone seeking a woman? The sound of sand upon sand under the Egyptian's feet seems sinister.

A woman should not walk in front of a man, but I dare not even turn to see him. My long black hair had tumbled from its womanly knot while I danced with delightful abandon on my exuberant journey. It's too late to cover it modestly with my shawl. Does the Egyptian perceive me as seductive? I quicken my pace as the sun begins sinking in the west.

We walk over the rise above the compound as dusk falls softly. Jeh-Jeh comes to meet us. I dare breathe deeply at last.

Jeh-Jeh thanks me with his kiss. Then he greets the Egyptian—in a tongue I do not understand. The imposing figure responds in the same tongue. I scamper to the women's quarters, freed of my arduous responsibility.

Jeh-Jeh and the Egyptian walk together to Jeh-Jeh's palatial dwelling, speaking heartily with one another like old friends. Why? Who is this man? Has my fearfulness been for nothing?

With my disarranged hair once more in its sedate knot, and my shepherdess garb changed to robes appropriate to breaking of bread with Jeh-Jeh and the stranger, I join my sisters and mothers on the women's side of the room, after bowing to the gods at the entrance.

Tonight there are no men except Jeh-Jeh and the Egyptian. Our brothers are on treks with goods from Midian for trade in other countries, while Spring's good weather contributes to their success.

The Egyptian and Jeh-Jeh continue a lively conversation in words they alone understand. Basemath supposes they speak in Hebrew, but Adah disagrees. I listen avidly. How I'd like to know what they are saying!

The slaves deliver large portions of meat and breads to the guest first and then a smaller amount for Jeh-Jeh. We women are next to receive our portions. My ears as alert as a sheep dog's, I eat slowly, while futilely trying to catch even one word of conversation from the men's side of the room.

I am the last to leave. The two men are still talking as I retire, mystified greatly by the events of this long day. From my mat in the women's quarters I see the glow from their candle. But my eyelids no longer can stay open.

Am I waking from a dream? Or is the Egyptian man already talking with Jeh-Jeh as we seven sisters leave with the sheep, this early morning? I had thought only women could chatter night and day. I am wrong!

The meal tonight is not festive. Again, the man and Jeh-Jeh carry on a spirited conversation. I never hear them laugh. The subject is evidently serious.

The Egyptian does not seem like a stranger to me anymore. I am finding myself attracted by his rather regal but non-condescending ways. Though not a young man, he sits straight as he speaks with Jeh-Jeh, his broad shoulders not slumping as older men's often do.

His face is expressive. His eyes are never cast down as if hiding something; instead they focus steadily on Jeh-Jeh as he speaks.

Suddenly I realize I am gazing at the Egyptian while my food is getting cold. My sisters are already leaving the table. For just a second, the man's eyes dart to me. I feel my cheeks blush. Quickly, I consume a few bites and hurry to the women's quarters, my thoughts confusing me greatly. Sleep refuses to overtake me until very late. Then I toss and turn, with dreams too vivid for comfort.

Dawn comes before I am rested. The sheep must quickly be led to pasture. As I'm snatching bread and cheese to eat as I go, the Egyptian man comes from the men's quarters and is ushered into Jeh-Jeh's presence. He does not bow to our gods. Perhaps his gods are hidden in the bag he carries.

The sun creeps over the horizon as the last ewe leaves the fold for the long day.

Even before we find good pasture, the jackals ambush the flock. With my slingshot I finish off one jackal. The rest of them run, tails between legs.

The lamb fallen from the brute's teeth lies helpless on the sand. I pick it up and cuddle the poor creature until it breathes no more. Then I dig a hole and bury it, hoping it is far enough under the soil that its odor won't call forth more sneaky predators. My sisters cheer my hitting an ugly target. Perhaps the rest of the day will be more calm for our sheep—and for us, their herders.

The afternoon's heat is nearly unbearable. We find no shade in the place where our sheep graze today, and no time to rest because of prowling wild animals. I suggest we take the flock to water and to the fold early. My sisters agree. Jeh-Jeh will understand.

Before slaves present the meals to us tonight, Jeh-Jeh stands to speak. He motions to the Egyptian at his side and announces, "His name is Moses." Then he introduces his wives and daughters by name to the man he called Moses. To each, Moses nods solemnly. I feel my ears turn red as he looks at me and nods. I hope my blush appears to be mere sunburn.

Jeh-Jeh asks that, after eating, we stay where we sit to hear something of import he must tell us. Then he sits down, and the slaves bring the food. For some reason, I find it very difficult to swallow, and I keep thinking about the Egyptian's look and nod when Jeh-Jeh introduced this daughter. My ears redden again.

Our meal is long over, but how can I sleep tonight? My mind is muddled with everything Jeh-Jeh had spoken about the man he called Moses.

I understand that Moses fled to Midian because of Pharaoh's murderous plot. For how many years has he wandered about in Midian? Why, at such a time, has he come to the well—and from the well to our compound?

Whatever did Jeh-Jeh mean about being very distantly related to Moses through Abraham? What kind of god was the god of Abraham and of his multitude of descendants? Is that god one to whom Moses bows?

And why has Jeh-Jeh decided, after only two days' communication with the Egyptian stranger, to assign Moses the task of caring for our flock?

My eldest sister is betrothed and must prepare for celebration when the groom returns with the bride-money. Jeh-Jeh's plan gives her adequate time, and allows us to aid her with weaving and embroidering. The one to whom she is promised is a man from royalty. She must be an elegant bride.

What could Jeh-Jeh have been thinking when he announced that he would give one of his daughters as a bride for Moses, after his years of servitude are over? Will my next eldest sister be that bride? Why do I care? Why?

Too soon I must pull myself from my rumpled bed and quickly dress. Last night Jeh-Jeh had assigned me to assist the Egyptian. How can the sheep know whom to follow unless one of us sisters begins to lead them out?

Why should I be the one?

In lessening darkness, I run to the gate of the fold. The Egyptian man is already here, the gate is open, and with his staff he has brought one ewe to the gate. The whole flock begins to follow, our well-trained sheep-dogs beside them. It's obvious I am not needed. A minimal smile silently thanks me for my offered assistance. Then he turns his full attention to the sheep.

For a foolish moment shall I wish I were one of the woolies? I trudge back towards the silence of the women's quarters, my ears beginning to burn because of what I am thinking. Then I catch the gleam of a candle from Jeh-Jeh's window, and turn aside to spend time with him, while everyone else still sleeps.

I clap my hands together thrice, a special signal between this daughter and her father. Jeh-Jeh welcomes me with a kiss. I sit at his feet and open my huge bundle of questions. Patiently he listens. Patiently he answers. I try to comprehend.

Yes, we are far-distant relatives. Our mutual patriarch, many generations ago, was the man Abraham. Abraham's god had promised him a son, but in his old age he failed to wait for the promised one and became father of Ishmael, his son by a slave woman. (Currently Ishmaelites and Midianites are competitors in trading, traveling often on the same routes. They are not friends.)

In fulfillment of his god's promise, Abraham's wife Sarah gave birth to Isaac. She was ninety and Abraham was one-hundred-years-old when Isaac was born, Jeh-Jeh says. Isaac became the father of Jacob, whose name was later changed to Israel. Jacob-Israel had twelve sons. Many thousands of Jacob's descendants are the present Israelites who, for years, have been cruelly treated slaves in Egypt.

How does Jeh-Jeh know all this history? Jeh-Jeh explains that, when he was young, he had studied in Egypt's most prestigious schools, so that he might become an excellent teacher to any children he might have in the future. I have profited! I thank him now.

Among his studies was the Hebrew language. Aha! So he and the Egyptian man were communicating in Hebrew. Basemath was right!

Jeh-Jeh tells me Moses is one of the Israelites who, somehow, became the adopted son of Egypt's princess and was in line to become Prince of Egypt. But he fled from Pharaoh and has wandered in Midian for many years.

Why did Jeh-Jeh say that we may be far-distant relatives? He goes on to explain that after Sarah died, Abraham married Keturah and became father of Midian, the Midian who founded our nation generations ago. I see, but somewhat skeptically.

Dawn is breaking. I hear noises as slaves get ready for the day's work. Women in our quarters waken and are dressing to oversee the female slaves in cleaning and carding. I must go now. I kiss Jeh-Jeh on each cheek and thank him heartily.

Prince of Egypt? No wonder that man carried himself regally and with dignity. How dare I consider the possibility of some day becoming ... I must cease such dreaming.

I, Zipporah, am merely one of the daughters of Prince Jehru, priest of Midian.

Marriage

Many suitors ask for me, but Jeh-Jeh always denies them their quest. He tells me again that I am much like my mother, whom he dearly loved, and so he will choose only the very best for me. A tear slips into his beard, and he turns quickly away.

Years slither and disappear like a lizard on a rock. After four years Moses brings the sheep back to our compound. The flock has more than doubled in size.

I, Zipporah, am given to Moses by priest Jethro to be his wife. Jeh-Jeh says to me, "I saved you for the best," and to Moses, in Hebrew, he says, "I saved the best for you." My sisters-in-law escort us with song and dance to the wedding chamber in a grove of trees.

While slaves shear heavy wool off hundreds of sheep, Moses and I enjoy our wedding week. How grateful I am that Jeh-Jeh spent many hours teaching me to understand and to speak Hebrew! Moses and I relished each day of talking and learning about one another's lives and aspirations.

At night he exulted as I danced for him in the moonlight.

The shorn flock with Moses, their shepherd, left yesterday to seek grazing by the streams which flow near the Horeb Range. Jeh-Jeh had chosen several of his most trusted slaves to accompany Moses. Moses is to teach them how to tend and protect the flock. When they have proven to be good shepherds under his authority and guidance,

Moses will divide the sheep into two flocks. I shall bow low and often before our gods, for success of that great endeavor.

In the past wonderful week, Moses tried to tell me about his god, but I failed to understand. How can a non-existent god hear? How can such a god give us what we ask? Our gods are visible. They stand before us when we pray. Obviously, they heard me when I prayed to be given to Moses as his bride. Today, after I bow in thanksgiving, I'll present my request for protection and health of my dear Moses.

My favorite among our gods is the one which has been artistically carved from fragrant wood; it provides its own incense as I bow. Some of the gods are covered with pure gold, standing on sturdy bases for our moments of worship. Some are made of ...

Suddenly I wonder: If we ourselves (or our artisans) have *made* the gods, how can those same gods listen to our requests and give us what we ask for? Can the god of Moses do so? Can his god be invisible and yet real? Moses thinks so. Why?

Two of our brothers' treks are finished for this spring. The others should soon be back. All brothers are needed for overseeing the slaves, in the planting of our wide plain. Jeh-Jeh's slaves are good workers when properly instructed.

One company which traded in Egypt reported the severe treatment of Israelite slaves under Pharaoh's ownership. Jeh-Jeh is never unkind to his slaves, and they respond with respect. (One who did not so respond was taken for sale on the next trading venture.)

I do not delay to eat this morning. Female slaves must be taught how to clean and card from the mountainous heaps of sheared wool, and then to spin, and begin to weave the beautiful cloth for which we are famous. I join my sisters to train them.

We are five now, my sisters and I. The two eldest have gone with their grooms to far lands. We five are the embroiderers in maroons and browns and gold threads. Our trader brothers will make good money from our artistry. Jeh-Jeh will be glad.

Recently, for several days, I cannot assist in teaching the female slaves. I feel ill and weak. Today my stomach does not wish any food. I prefer only to sleep.

Basemath has been observing me. Secretly she whispers, "I think I shall be called 'Grandmother' in a few more months!" I am overjoyed. To be carrying Moses' child makes me want to dance and sing. But I am too ill to try.

At long last comes the wonderful day! I hold Moses' tiny son at my breast. How sweet he is! I think he looks like Moses—without the beard, of course. But his hair is like mine. His name? At the next shearing time, his own father shall name him. Until then I simply dub him "Little Mo".

Little Mo is an Israelite. This is the eighth day, circumcision day for Israelite males. Jeh-Jeh knows what Moses would have wanted him to do, and he does it. Little Mo cries and cries. I cry with him. In a few days he will be healed, and shall be a proven Israelite.

As he grows, I will tell little Mo about his father. I want him and Moses to know one another. How can it be with Moses far away? Jeh-Jeh adores this grandson, but he dares not take Moses' place in Little Mo's heart, he knows.

It is difficult for me to endure these long years until shearing time. Then our little family will have days to be together. With emotional issues, such as longing for my man and my lack of patience, our gods do not help. Could the god of Moses?

Little Mo hears a sound as of distant thunder. His left eyebrow raises as Jeh-Jeh's does when he's puzzled. I say, "Let's run up the hill and see what's happening." Together we go to the rim of our compound. There we see a moving sea of sheep! I dance and shout and laugh and cry and dance some more, and Little Mo tries to mimic my dance.

One shepherd breaks away from the flock and hurries toward us. "Little Mo!" I say, with great joy, "Here comes your father!"

Moses scoops Little Mo into one arm and hugs me with the other. "Gershom," he says. "His name is Gershom, for I have been an exile in a strange land, but in this exile my God has given me a wife and a son. Praise to Him!"

With two large flocks, shearing requires more than a week. Moses and Gershom and I enjoy each day. Gershom quickly becomes attached to his father, who loves him tremendously. Moses has been making up games for the two to play together, while at the same time, trying to prepare Gershom—and himself—for parting when shearing is finished.

Sometimes I hear Moses speak aloud to his invisible god about his little son. Does his god hear? Is Moses simply a mystic like me—or does he speak to something real but not seeable?

Will our gods be angry if I should try to bow to his god?

Too soon, the huge flocks are gone from the compound to faraway grazing lands. Jeh-Jeh seems much pleased with Moses' prowess in educating the slaves to be excellent shepherds. The sheep have multiplied under his administration, and the slaves appear joyful with their elevated positions as deputies for Jeh-Jeh. Everyone seems happy—everyone except me. Separation is very painful!

Gershom continues growing like a weed, vigorous and healthy, perhaps like his father at this age. Moses, however, was growing up in Pharaoh's palace. Gershom has wide open spaces in which to romp and explore, turning over rocks to look for bugs, climbing into small trees to see birds' nests with their colorful eggs, and playing boisterously with two cousins who are almost the same size as he.

A Burning Bush

Again I am with child. This time I have a good appetite and am not sick at my stomach, or ill at all. I'm glad—for another child growing within me, and for feeling well. I can weave and embroider with my remaining sisters and my sisters-in-law.

Moses would be happy if only I could tell him. Our baby will be born before shearing time comes again. Waiting is almost more than I can bear. May the gods help me!

Only six days old, the second little Mo is a voracious eater. In my space in the women's quarters I try to satisfy his appetite, but I am not successful. I carry him to suckle one of the goats.

Suddenly Gershom begins screaming, "Mo-mo! Mo-mo! Mo-mo!" and runs like an shooting arrow toward—

It cannot be! Moses! My dearest Moses!

Gershom hugs Moses' legs tightly until his father grabs the little boy's hands and swings him round and round, both of them laughing with glee. Finally he sets his son down, takes his hand, and together they run to me.

Gently Moses lifts his newly-born son into his strong arms, smiles lovingly as the baby wails, and pronounces, "His name shall be Eliezer, for God has helped me."

This day, when Moses speaks, my eyes are filled with questions. Moses' answers produces only more questions.

He says he was overseeing the shepherds, who were herding their flocks on the back side of the desert, near Mount Horeb, when he saw a bush that was on fire but was not consumed. I tell Moses that I know those bushes. When they are covered with blooms they look almost to be on fire.

But this is not the season for them to bloom. Moses insists there was a flame of fire within the bush. I tell him he has a great imagination! He ignores my remark and continues with a fanciful tale. He had left the flocks and gone close to the bush, to see why it kept burning but wasn't burned to ashes, he says.

Suddenly, he says, God spoke to him from inside the bush, and called him by name—twice.

A god who speaks? Our gods do nothing but stand there and accept our worship. No one has ever heard any of them speak. Has Moses had sunstroke? I humor him by continuing to listen as he rambles on about some god who actually spoke to him. But I am frightened—Moses really seems to believe what he's telling me!

He says a voice told him to take off his sandals, because he was standing on holy ground. Moses hid his face, he says, because he was afraid to look at what he was sure was God. That voice he called God told him to go back to Egypt and bring the Israelites out from their bondage.

Moses says he argued with the One he calls God. How could he tell the Hebrews *Who* had sent him to rescue them? He says, very earnestly, that God said to tell them His name is *I AM*.

Eliezer begins crying loud and then louder, and I cannot hear all that Moses is saying. I think he said he had talked with Jeh-Jeh who told him to "go in peace." I myself can have no peace until my baby gets back to the goat and gets his belly full.

Tonight, Moses tries to tell me more. I find his words mysterious and strange. One thing I understand, however, is that we will soon be leaving on a long trip. I must pack well for my children and myself.

To Egypt

The poor donkey has a heavy load. At times Gershom walks proudly with his Mo-mo, who even lets him carry his rod, briefly. The goat, on a long rope behind us, finds grass and weeds to eat, and provides the children with plenty of milk. So far the journey has not been too difficult.

This night I am too exhausted to dance in the moonlight for Moses. While we tried to sleep at the encampment *last* night, Moses moaned and flailed about, gasping for air so dreadfully that I thought he was dying. With one last gulp of breath, he cried out that he had disobeyed God, by failing to circumcise Eliezer on the eighth day, and so he must die.

I grabbed the sharpest piece of flint-stone I could find, sliced off my baby boy's foreskin, and threw it at Moses' feet. "You are a husband of blood to me," I said, angrily. Moses breathed deeply, stopped writhing, and fell sound asleep.

My baby cried a long time, and I cried with him. What will the one he calls God do next? He seems ultra-demanding and impossible to obey. Yet Moses chooses to honor Him. I do not understand.

Moses' elder brother Aaron meets him near the mount, and together we make our way into Egypt. We are guided into the section named Goshen, where the Israelites have lived for more than four centuries.

We are welcomed at the home of Moses' sister Miriam by Amram and Jochabed, their parents. They are overjoyed to see Moses again after nearly forty years! But they seem uncomfortable with me. My two sons are Israelites, but I am not. Their God is not my god.

Aaron and Moses call a special meeting, for the leaders of the twelve tribes of Israel. They gather by torchlight tonight, hearing through Aaron's lips what Moses tells him God has spoken: that God cares about them in their misery and will deliver them from Egypt, and take them to the land promised to Abraham as a possession forever.

After years and years of cruel slavery, the leaders don't believe. But when they see the signs God gave Moses for proof, they bow—to an unseen god—and worship *with praise* to that god.

Of course, I am not part of the meeting; but even as weary as I am from our long journey, I crouch behind a bush in the courtyard and listen secretly until the baby begins to squirm and wake in my arms. I must not be discovered. In darkness I slip away and take Eliezer to the goat to suckle.

Back inside the house, I put dry clothing on my little one and lie down to sleep beside him.

When I awake, Moses has already eaten breakfast. He tells me that Aaron and he will confront Pharaoh today. He says God told him Pharaoh will be stubborn and refuse to let the people of Israel go, but God will use the stubbornness to bring glory to Himself. Through many miracles, Moses tells me, Pharaoh will finally acknowledge God.

My Moses is a dreamer. How could there really be a god who speaks? My gods, through our magicians, can do signs and miracles—which I have always suspected are just very clever tricks! Moses thinks his God can do genuine signs and miracles to prove Who He is.

Not only does he believe that his God does miracles, but also he seems certain that his God *speaks*!

Tonight, Moses says Pharaoh insists the Israelites are just lazy. He orders his overseers to make them work much harder and faster, and to beat those who don't meet their quotas for each day.

The king who had plotted, forty years ago, to have Moses killed, is dead. The present king is even more harsh and cruel than the former one. He doesn't realize that the harder the Hebrew people are forced to work, the stronger their bodies are becoming.

Moses and Aaron go back to Pharaoh early in the morning and demand that the Israelites be allowed to go out of the land to worship God. Moses says Pharaoh snorted at the demand. He didn't know their god, he shouted, and they could not go. They must work even harder!

Moses says he and Aaron warned Pharaoh about what will happen to him and his people if he continues to resist God, but the king turns a deaf ear. He thinks God cannot do anything. Moses says Pharaoh will soon have to give up, because God will work very powerfully against the king and his officials.

Pharaoh's Folly

Moses leaves very early this morning. He and Aaron meet Pharaoh at the river. With his rod Aaron strikes the river, and suddenly all the water in the river and streams and even in waterpots turns to blood.

Must we bathe in blood? How can we quench thirst? With shovels we dig near the river to find fresh water. Pharaoh doesn't seem to care, Moses says. He declares that his magicians can do the same thing.

After seven days, Aaron and Moses go back to Pharaoh. They tell him God wants His people to go away and worship Him, and if Pharaoh won't let them go, God will send frogs everywhere in the land. Pharaoh laughs! Who is God? He says he doesn't know Him and won't let the people go.

Today, frogs are everywhere! At first Gershom tries to play with them, but there are so many he can't even run without falling over them. They are on our table, in our cooking pot, and even in our beds. When I try to wrap Eliezer in his blanket, I also wrap two frogs!

I understand that frogs are among Egypt's gods. How can they bow to a creature that won't sit still for one moment? I prefer Moses' invisible god to a million visible ones like these ugly hopping things!

What must Pharaoh think now? Maybe he likes to sit on frogs while he eats frog soup. I don't. And why must the Israelites—and I with them—partake in Pharaoh's punishment? What kind of god causes that?

Pharaoh wants Moses to get rid of the frogs. When? "Tomorrow!" So when Moses goes to Pharaoh in the morning, the frogs leave, except those in the river. The rest of them die. I help Amram gather up the ones at this house and courtyard. They're lying in great piles, and the stench is terrible. Moses tells us the smell of dead frogs is all over Egypt. I hope Pharaoh enjoys the stink!

If Pharaoh thinks he can bargain with the invisible God who speaks to Moses, he is gravely mistaken, judging from what Moses tells me. Today Aaron shows the king what God will do next because he refuses to let the people go.

He strikes the ground with his rod, and the dust turns into tiny insects swarming all over Egypt. No one can get away from them. The bugs get into our hair, gather around the baby's mouth when he eats, and crawl all over our bodies. We itch and scratch frantically.

Moses says Pharaoh's magicians can't duplicate the miracle. They tell the king, "This is the finger of God!" He scoffs—and itches, I hope. And he makes sort of a promise, and then breaks it again.

After a day or two, a new miracle shakes the nation. But this time the Hebrews are spared. Millions and millions of flies cover the rest of Egypt, all the people and animals alike. God tells Moses that He wants the Egyptians to see that He is the real God, and so there are no flies in all of Goshen.

The gods to which I used to bow could never have done such a miracle. I'm beginning to question ...

Pharaoh's stubborn resistance to all the warnings Aaron and Moses give him brings death by pestilence to cattle, horses, camels, and oxen. Even such disaster doesn't break him.

And neither does the awful plague of boils on all the people. The magicians cannot stand up to try their magic because they also are covered with boils.

Those disasters do not touch anyone in Goshen, Moses knows, because God makes an invisible line between Goshen and the rest of Egypt.

Hmm! An invisible God makes an invisible line to spare His people. The invisible God seems more real than my gods back in Midian. I've never seen my gods do anything like the miracles God has been doing here.

Moses says God is using Pharaoh's stubborn heart to show the world God's power. Aaron is there now warning the king to have his people find shelter for themselves and animals because of what God will do the next day. Some people believe.

In Goshen this morning the sun shines brightly with not a cloud in the sky. But we hear tremendous thunder and see brilliant flashes of lightning over the rest of Egypt. Moses sees later the devastation of the land from hail, the likes of which no one can remember and probably never shall see again.

Cowardly, Pharaoh has huddled in his palace, sending some of his aides to try to rescue animals. Aides and animals die. Crops and fruit trees are shredded. Egypt is empty, like a deserted nation, Moses says, with great heaps of hailstones covering all the land. Surely many days will pass before all the ice melts away.

Some of his servants plead for the king to heed the warnings of Moses and Aaron. He remains arrogantly defiant. Instead of allowing the Hebrews to go and serve their God, the king cruelly forces them to work even harder, with no straw left in all of Egypt to mix with the clay for making bricks.

There may be more disasters until Pharaoh says the Hebrews may go. Moses and Aaron have gone to the palace with dire warnings from the God of Israel. I do not understand this invisible but superbly powerful God of Moses. Having seen the evidence of many miracles, I begin to believe his God is real, but I'm afraid my gods will be angry. I want to talk with Moses about my fear when he returns.

Tonight, Moses tells me he and Aaron had gone again to Pharaoh. They told him if he refused to humble himself before God and let the people go, God will send locusts to all the land of Egypt—tomorrow.

The spelt and wheat had not yet grown through the soil when the hail destroyed the barley and flax. Now those later crops are flourishing with the moisture from melted hail, Moses says, and some trees are sprouting new leaves. But locusts will come and devour anything green that exists in every field and orchard.

Pharaoh's servants beg the king to let the people go, saying, "Don't you know that Egypt is being destroyed?" But Pharaoh's heart becomes even more hardened. He drives Moses and Aaron out of his presence.

Then Moses stretches out his rod over all of Egypt, and a strong east wind begins to blow. It blows all day and all night. Probably Pharaoh thinks everything is going his way. But this morning the sky grows dark—with locusts. And, as Moses had told the king, so many locusts cover all of Egypt that people can't even see the ground beneath their feet.

Locusts leave not one bit of green. At last Pharaoh, in haste, calls for Moses and Aaron and tells them, "I have sinned against the God you serve, and against you also. Please forgive my sin and ask your God to take away this death."

Moses tells me that he went out of the palace and prayed, and that the Lord sent a very strong west wind which blew all the locusts into the Red Sea until not one locust existed in the entire land.

Again the wicked king's heart hardens, and he refuses to let the Israelites leave Egypt to worship God as God chooses to be worshiped.

Moses says he lifted his hand toward heaven, and thick darkness now covers all of Egypt, darkness so deep it's actually felt. People can't see one another and scarcely dare to move. How can they care for children whom they cannot see? How can they find food to eat?

In Goshen there is plenty of light. Children are playing as they normally do, and meals are being prepared as usual. Moses says in Egypt the darkness will last for three days! He tells me the most honored and most powerful god of Egypt is Ra, the sun god. The most powerful god cannot stop the darkness? Hah!

After three days Pharaoh sends for Moses and tells him the Hebrews may go, but they must leave all their flocks and herds here. Moses says God wants some of the livestock for sacrifices, and not one will be left behind. The king is furious.

Forcefully, Moses tells him that, if he will not yield, Egypt will soon be stricken by God with the last and most unimaginably terrible plague, for at midnight the firstborn of every person and animal shall die. There shall be a great cry throughout all the land, such wailing as has never been heard before nor will ever be again.

Pharaoh stubbornly does not heed the very serious warning, but yells at Moses to get out and never come back.

Moses is highly respected by the servants of Pharaoh and by most Egyptian people. He could choose to take his lawful place as Prince of Egypt. Instead, he chooses rather to suffer for the God he worships by going with the Hebrews, the people of Israel. I would not understand unless I had seen the great power of his God. Now I wish I were Hebrew. But I'm a foreigner. Where do I fit?

Passover

I have cooperated with Amram and Jochabed to care for the lamb chosen the tenth day of this month. For each family a lamb without any defect has been taken from the flock. Gershom has helped take care of our lamb. But, as Moses had told the leader of every Hebrew tribe, the lamb is to be killed at twilight on the fourteenth day of this month.

Today is the fourteenth day. At twilight, Moses holds Gershom in his arm when Amram slits the lamb's throat and drains its blood into a basin. Then my dear man has his son help him dip hyssop into the basin and swab the two doorposts and the lintel of the house with the blood of the lamb.

Carefully, he explains to Gershom that God will pass through the land tonight, and when He sees the blood on the lintel and doorposts of any house, He will pass over that house, and no one there will die. (He does not tell him that in Egyptian houses, at midnight, every firstborn son will die as judgment on all the gods of Egypt.)

Gershom stays awake while we roast the lamb and prepare to eat, but he's too sleepy to eat more than a small piece of the meat and a bit of flat bread. I dress him for a long journey and put him to bed. He sleeps soundly, not hearing the shrieks and wails that rise from Egypt at midnight.

The rest of us are fully dressed, sandals included. We eat in haste, for we are to leave quickly. Jochabed and Miriam and I have packed as much as we and the donkeys can carry. With our packs are heavy bags of gold, silver, and precious gem-stones, given to us by the

Egyptians, all tucked into the cart between spinning-wheel and loom and clothing and miscellaneous items.

The livestock is well fed, ready to follow us as we leave Egypt for the land promised to Abraham centuries ago. Tonight the Hebrews are to be free at last!

Moses names this night the *Passover* and says it must be celebrated each year by the Israelites as an everlasting remembrance.

Screams and loud cries continue from homes in Egypt. Pharaoh sends for Moses and Aaron, and curses and yells at them, telling them to get out of the land immediately and to take all their animals with them.

Then the hypocrite adds, "And bless me also."

Long before daybreak, every tribe marches toward Succoth, about six-hundred-thousand men in all, besides women and children, plus large flocks and herds. The people of Israel (Hebrews) celebrate with shouts and songs. Free at last! Free at last! After four hundred and thirty years, free at last!

Jochabed's Story

The stars are bright above Succoth tonight. The great host of Jacob's descendants, twelve tribes having marched orderly all day, are now peaceful and at rest, no longer slaves. Moses' God has set them free.

In the flicker of the dying campfire embers, Jochabed holds little Eliezer and gazes long at his face. A tear trickles down her wrinkled cheek, but a smile is on her lips.

"He looks very much like the baby boy I loved eighty years ago," she says softly. The wicked king had given orders to kill every Israelite male baby. Aaron was three then and no longer a baby. But how could she save this little one?

"I prayed to the God Who hears," my mother-in-law tells me, "and He helped me make a basket that could float. I put my precious child into the basket, shut the lid, and laid him in the reeds along the river."

The princess saw him and wanted him for her own. She said that because she had drawn him out of the water, she would name him Moses.

I gasp! I have never heard this before.

Miriam is sitting with us, and she takes up the story. "The princess said she wanted him to be her child," she begins. "Then I popped up from my hiding place in the reeds and told her I could get a nurse for him."

Another tear rolls down Jochabed's face. "The princess hired me to nurse my own baby! She didn't know I was also teaching him about God. Yes, he grew up in a palace, but also in our humble home, where he learned to worship the God Who hears."

"And now," says Jochabed, "God has spoken to Moses and made him a powerful leader. We Israelites must follow God, with Moses as our shepherd."

Gently she lays my sleeping baby next to his father and Gershom. I slip under the blanket beside them. "God," I say, "Do You really hear? I want to tell You I'm happy about this story tonight." But I can't say anything else.

The Red Sea

We camp under the stars again tonight after a long day of marching. We dare not expect too much from the flocks and herds, and so we stop, gather our families together, and eat the evening meals. As I fall asleep, a soft breeze plays sweet music for my ears.

Surely these Hebrews, at last freed from slavery, are eager to get to the land God promised to Abraham and his descendants forever. Why can they not simply take the shortest way to that land? Moses tells me that God knows the people might be afraid of the war-loving Philistines on the route and actually choose to go back to slavery! And so, instead, they must travel for many days through the wilderness.

We begin trekking again early this morning, but I am puzzled. It seems to me that we are turning around instead of going forward.

We camp now at Pihaharoth near the sea. Before us is a high pillar of cloud which we follow wherever it moves. The wondrous cloud stays with us each day and gives soft light all night.

Surely our journey will take many tiring days, some more tiring than this one perhaps. For a lullaby as I snuggle down to sleep, I hear the slap of waves on the shore of the Red Sea.

Horror of horrors!

This morning we hear a fearsome noise. Far away we see the Egyptians racing toward us with chariots and horses and all the army. Pharaoh is not only crazed with grief over the death of his firstborn son but also furious over the Hebrews' leaving. And so he will try to overtake us—and there is no way to escape because of the sea!

Former slaves keep screaming that they would have been better off to have stayed in Egypt rather than die brutally in this wilderness. The terrified Hebrews cry out against Moses, and Moses cries out to God.

The cloud moves quickly from before our ranks and forms behind us, blinding the Egyptians with light during the day and with fire all night, so that the Egyptians and Israel's people are completely separated by Moses' God.

Although we cannot see the huge army, we hear the clashing of swords and the snorting of horses. We also hear the sound of a strong east wind which blows all night. The wind separates the waters of the sea into two parts, forming walls on either side and drying up the ground in the very middle of the sea.

While the Egyptians are stymied from approaching, all Israelites—men, women, children, and animals—hurry the long distance between walls of water toward safety on the eastern seashore.

Moses' God lifts the cloud away from the Egyptians. Horses and chariots and soldiers come roaring into the path the Israelites are treading. God loosens the chariot wheels so they cannot keep going forward, but neither can they go back.

As the last Israelite arrives on the shore, the waters return in full force. Every Egyptian of Pharaoh's army dies. Their bodies in full armor wash up on the seashore alongside dead horses and mangled chariots.

The sight makes me shudder. But the people at last fully believe the Lord, and Moses, God's special servant. They begin to sing and shout with great joy. Miriam with her timbrel and other women with timbrels sing and dance. (Will it be all right if I join them?)

All peoples around us will know how powerful is Israel's God when they hear about His triumph over the Egyptians. I myself must acknowledge that none of my gods could have done such a spectacular thing as has the God of Moses.

I would like to know Him, the One Who hears and speaks, but I am afraid of Him. It seems He knows everything. If so, He knows me. He knows I have bowed to other gods, and have done many things for which He likely would disapprove. I want to talk with Moses, but he is too busy for talking now. I must simply watch and listen.

Wilderness Provisions

I am glad to get far away from the dead Egyptians by the Red Sea, but I don't enjoy plodding with the Hebrews deep into this Shur Wilderness.

This is our third warm and dusty day, and already it seems too long. Even the animals are weary and have slowed considerably. My sisters and I know the desert offers little to drink, with many miles between wells or streams, and so I'm well-prepared. I've loaded our donkey with bags of water, enough for Moses and Gershom and little Eliezer—and for Jochabed and Amram who can't go on if we don't find water soon.

We near Marah. As the sun is setting, we see its gleam on the waters! Almost everyone rushes to drink. Quickly, they spit out the water! "It's bitter!" they cry out, angrily complaining to Moses. "What shall we drink?"

Moses cries out to God, and God shows him a tree to throw into the waters. The waters are healed and instantly become sweet. Moses tells the people God was testing them there. He says God promises that if they will diligently heed His voice and obey Him, He will keep the diseases of the Egyptians from them. Moses assures the people that God says, "I am the Lord Who heals."

Thirsts quenched, animals watered and fed, and meals made and eaten, Hebrews, and the mixed multitude among them, sleep in contentment, with the mysterious cloud giving light until the morning comes again.

I've been wishing Moses will have energy to play for a short while with Gershom, but he's completely exhausted. He scarcely finishes eating before he falls asleep. I'd like to ask him some questions, but not tonight.

At Elim we camp for a few days, under seventy palm trees and beside twelve wells of water. How refreshing! And no complaining!

No complaining doesn't last after we leave Elim and head toward Sinai. We've been out of Egypt for just one month, and the Hebrews seem to have forgotten that they had been slaves for many years. They begin grumbling about the same old camp food. They say they want plenty of meat and bread like they used to have in the land of Egypt.

They moan to Moses and Aaron that the Lord should have killed them in Egypt instead of bringing them out into this wilderness to starve them to death. Moses tells me what the Lord had told him then.

To the angry people, Moses says, "The Lord hears your complaints *against Him*. Who are we, that you complain against us?" He and Aaron remind the children of Israel that it was God the Lord Who brought them out of the land of their slavery.

Moses bids Aaron to call the whole congregation to come near before the Lord, and he tells Aaron what to say to the people. I listen in silence. While Aaron is speaking, I gaze toward the wilderness. In the cloud I see what must be the glory of the Lord! Everyone looks—and stands in awe.

Moses tells the people that God had heard their complaint against Him. (Are we ashamed? I am! And I'm not one of those who claim to worship the God of Abraham.)

Moses goes on to tell us that God says, "At twilight you shall eat meat, and in the morning you shall be filled with bread. Thus you shall know that I am the Lord your God."

Meat and bread? How can that happen? It's a desert place where we'll camp this evening. But if Moses says God told him so, I will believe it. Moses hears from the God Who speaks. Jochabed, Amram, Miriam, Moses, and I, with our little boys, will prepare to eat meat at tonight's meal, and there will be bread in the morning. God has promised!

At twilight quails begin coming. They cover the whole camp. There is enough tasty meat to satisfy everyone's hunger. God did it, just as He said He would. My gods could not speak and certainly couldn't provide meat for 600,000 men plus many women and children. The God Who speaks somehow made the quails come. No complaining now!

Probably the quails have been migrating, and we have been thus fed. Tonight we sleep easily, full and contented. But bread can't fly. How can there be bread tomorrow?

Early this morning, I lift the tent flap and look out. Dew lies all over the camp. As the sun rises, the dew lifts but leaves a small round something which looks almost like frost on the ground. When the Hebrews come out of their tents they are astonished by what they see. They ask each other, "Manna? What is it?"

Moses tells them this is the bread the Lord had promised to give them. He gives instructions about how much to gather according to the number of persons in each tent. He says they must gather enough for one day and must not save any of it overnight.

I'm as skeptical as the next person, but I'm sure Moses hears from his God, and so we gather only one day's supply for our family, before the hot sun melts it away. I cook it in goat broth. It's delicious! And I'm tempted to save some, but in my mind I hear Moses' voice saying, "This is what the Lord commands."

But what can we eat tomorrow?

Tomorrow has come. Women begin shrieking in their tents. "It stinks! There are worms crawling in it! What has Moses done to us now?"

Moses is angry. He had told them clearly what God commanded, but some people disobeyed. Perhaps they think God doesn't see what they do—or that Moses doesn't know what he's talking about.

Moses' God must love even rebels. He sends manna again this morning.

Moses tells the leaders to be sure that every day families gather just enough for one day, except on the sixth day. On that day they should gather twice as much, because the seventh day will be a day of rest, a holy Sabbath for the Lord, and they must not work.

I baked manna yesterday and boiled some for today's Sabbath. As Moses' God had promised, it doesn't stink or breed worms. Those who disobeyed yesterday went out this morning and found no manna. I don't feel sorry for them. They must learn God means what He says! (Well, I do give some of mine to the little child in the neighboring tent.)

The God Who speaks tells Moses to say to Aaron, "Fill a pot with manna and lay it up before the Lord for generations to come, so that they may see the bread with which I fed you in the wilderness when I brought you out of Egypt." Sounds odd to me, but Aaron does it.

After the Sabbath we begin our journey again, as the Lord commanded. Usually along our way we find streams for our refreshment. Today we tramped through hot desert sands with no springs or creeks. Everyone is dreadfully thirsty. Even the livestock walk with heads low, tongues hanging out.

Toward evening, we catch sight of a small settlement some distance ahead. Surely they have water. We walk a bit faster.

We arrive in Rephidim, where only a few people remain. There is no water to drink. But night will soon overtake us, and so we must camp here.

Angry people yell at Moses, "Give us water! Why did you bring us out of Egypt to kill us and our children and livestock with thirst?" They begin to pick up stones. I huddle with Gershom and Eliezer in the tent while the crowd gets more and more angry. I hear Moses cry out to God.

I cannot hear the answer of the God Who speaks, but obviously Moses hears. Aaron and Moses call some of the elders of Israel to go immediately with them to the rock at Horeb. In front of all the elders, Moses strikes the rock with his rod, and water comes gushing out. It cascades down the rock and forms a huge pool. Everyone has enough for families and livestock for as long as we camp at Rephidim.

Moses names the place "Meribah" because of the contention of the Israelites, and because they tempted the Lord, saying, "Is the Lord among us or not?" Seems to me they should ask, "Are we with the Lord or not?" I guess they already know the answer!

The children are asleep, and so are Jochabed and Amram. Tonight Moses and I have a wee bit of time to walk together under the stars. He explains to me what God had told him today, that the Lord would stand before him there on the rock at Horeb. Then he should strike the rock with the rod of God in his hand.

The people don't see God. They see Moses. He thinks they are beginning to elevate him. He's just a man, he says, and dares not accept their adulation. He wants them to know the God of Abraham and Isaac and Jacob, the God who created everything and can do everything when He chooses.

He especially wants me to know his God, he says softly. I say I want to know Him and obey Him. Moses is very happy with my words.

We walk in silence for a while, and then Moses tells me that he talked with a shepherd of one of Jeh-Jeh's flocks. It's almost shearing time, when all the flocks will be returning to my father's compound. Moses wants me to take our sons and go with that shepherd and the flock.

Home again! The thought brings tears to my eyes. Yes, I'd like to go, but I don't want to be away from Moses. He's the finest man my wise father could ever have chosen for me. How can I leave him?

While Moses holds me close, he tells me he wants me to go—go and tell his father-in-law all I've observed God do. Also, he says, there is another reason: Amalek is preparing for war against the Israelites. Moses urges me to leave *tomorrow* so that his sons and his precious wife won't be in danger.

I'll do what Moses requests. Before morning, he will make a connection with Jeh-Jeh's shepherd. In order to leave in safety, I quickly pack and load the donkey. We slip away in the dark so that none of Amalek's men will see us. Moses weeps as he says goodbye to his sleepy little ones, and to me.

He asks God to go with us on our trip back to Jeh-Jeh with the shepherd and his flock of sheep. Moses says I can talk to God myself, and God will hear. God will hear *me*? Who am *I*?

Back Home

As we travel slowly with Jeh-Jeh's large flock, I tell Gershom how my sisters and I used to herd the gentle woolly creatures. I point out some of the places where the sheep grazed. I tell him how I stopped the jackal with my slingshot one day.

Camping under the stars at night, surrounded by sheep, seems natural to me, but to Gershom it's like a different world. And to me, somehow, it feels this world existed much longer ago than it really did. In just a few months so much has happened that my mind fumbles to think about it.

This evening we arrive at the well. I tell my son that it was here I met his Mo-mo. I say I was afraid of him at first. He was tall and strong and important-looking. But I had to lead that strange man to his grandfather Jeh-Jeh's home even if I was scared.

While the flock is drinking, with little Eliezer safe in the donkey's pack, Gershom and I walk together to the terebinth tree. I show him my mother's grave and the special stone I put there as my love gift. I try to explain why this grave is important to me, but my little son doesn't understand.

Leading the donkey, we walk the rest of the way to Jeh-Jeh's compound. Gershom remembers his grandfather and runs into his arms. I must wait my turn!

Jeh-Jeh is overjoyed to see us again. Lovingly he holds Eliezer, but Eliezer is hungry and cries. His goat nanny has had triplets recently, but she still has milk for Eliezer, too. Tonight he's much more satisfied than I've been able to make him since we left here. He should grow fatter now and stronger, besides. I'm very grateful.

Basemath and everyone in the women's quarters are excited to see me. We talk and talk until sleep takes over—for everyone except me.

Jeh-Jeh wants to know all that has happened. My brothers from two trading treks had brought back startling news about Egypt and the Israelites. I have lived through it. We talk until I can't stay awake any longer.

For the ten days while sheep are being sheared, Jeh-Jeh listens eagerly to my story. I tell him about the miracles of the God Who speaks. None softened Pharaoh's heart so he would let the Hebrews go. I tell him about the plagues Moses' God inflicted upon the Egyptian people, and I tell him how the Israelites were separated from the Egyptians during the worst of those plagues.

I try to explain the night of Passover when the blood of a lamb was applied to lintel and doorposts so the death angel would pass over that house, while all the firstborn Egyptian males died at midnight.

He is grateful, he says, that our family obeyed the command of the invisible God. If we hadn't, Gershom would have been buried in a grave in Egypt instead of romping around with his cousins in the yard now.

Jeh-Jeh had heard about the crossing at the Red Sea. He says all the nations around are afraid of the Israelites who have a God Who can do such great things.

He asks many questions about Moses' God. I tell him Moses actually hears the One Who speaks—hears His voice. Jeh-Jeh is greatly puzzled. His left eyebrow lifts for a moment, and then he wants to know more.

He says Moses' God sounds like the God our ancestor Abraham knew—a wonderful God. He understands why I no longer bow to the gods, as I enter his door. He agrees that his gods neither hear nor speak.

He tells me he wants to know the God about whom I'm talking. He says he believes me, but he wants to see for himself.

After shearing is finished, and all the fields are planted, he wants to meet Moses again. He has heard that Amalek's army has been defeated and won't be a danger to us now.

Eliezer likes to crawl on Jeh-Jeh's carpet. He has gotten almost chunky since he's being well-fed, and he smiles toothlessly whenever his grandfather picks him up. Camping in the desert has not been very good for him. Several babies have been buried as we have traveled, but Moses' God has surely kept His eye on little Eliezer.

Gershom is happy as a lark here with his cousins. He's an outgoing youngster who makes friends with other children as we travel. When we are in the camps, Moses tries to play with his young son as much as possible. He tells him stories, too, stories about Abraham and Isaac and Jacob. The story Gershom likes best is the story about Jacob's son Joseph.

When his father tells him stories, he acts out the various parts. He makes Israelite characters very real to Gershom—and to me, also!

How can it be that I'm the mother of two Israelite children? Prince Jethro, priest of Midian, is my father. I'm an alien among the Israelites. Yes, I can speak and understand Hebrew, but I look different than the Israelite women and have an accent, I know. Because of Moses, I'm tolerated by other campers, but I'm definitely not one of them.

Why in the world am I thinking such thoughts? I suppose it's because I feel "at home" here where I grew up. I am not "at home" in the camps. Jochabed and Amram have taken me in as the wife of their son, and I feel as if I "belong" when I'm with them. But what will I feel when they are no longer alive?

Moses said I could talk to You, God, and You will hear me. Maybe I'll never feel "at home" unless I can hear Your voice and know that I belong in Your family.

Here I am, God. I'm listening. Please give me ears to recognize Your voice.

Jethro and Moses

Jeh-Jeh on his camel and I with two donkeys are on our way to see Moses. My heart skips beats when I think of being with my good husband again. I know his boys have missed him, too.,

Somehow, it has been heard that Prince Jethro is coming to meet Moses, bringing our sons and me with him. Moses hurries out to meet his father-in-law, bows, and kisses him. He swings Gershom in circles, and they both laugh aloud with happiness. Then little Eliezer wakes up and reaches for his father. My turn must wait until it's just the two of us.

Moses and Jeh-Jeh talk excitedly all the way back to the camp. I listen. Jeh-Jeh praises the Lord for the great things He has done in delivering the Israelites from the Egyptians. "Now I know," he says in unusual awe, "that the Lord is greater than all gods!"

At last at camp, my father makes a burnt offering in sacrifice to God. Aaron and all the elders of Israel come before the Lord to eat bread with Jeh-Jeh. He is not treated as an alien but as one who trusts Israel's God. Of course it's a man-only event. I ache to be with Moses, but I must wait until the feasting is over and night has fallen.

This camp at Rephidim is spread out wide. Everything is quiet now—except for snores, of course. Moses and I sit on a large rock in the moonlight and talk in whispers of things in our hearts. I love this man God Himself has chosen for me, and I am loved by him.

In the morning, as seems to be common, Moses is besieged by dozens and dozens of Israelites who bring difficulties for him to hear and judge. He is to tell them what God wants them to do in each conflict. Jeh-Jeh watches and listens for two or three hours. Then he says to me that Moses will wear himself out totally unless he quits being both complaint-post and judge for everyone all day long.

He has heard how Amalek's army was defeated while Moses held high the rod of God. He knows that Aaron and Hur, on either side of Moses, lifted up his hands when his arms got too weary to continue holding up the rod. Jeh-Jeh says to Moses that he must have help instead of being sole arbitrator for the disgruntled. There must be others to "hold up his arms", he says, and he gives Moses good advice.

I overhear the conversation, and I'm grateful for Jeh-Jeh's wisdom. If God so commands, he says, Moses must stand before God for the people, teaching them God's statutes and laws and the way they must walk and the work they must do. But he must not do everything himself.

My father recommends that Moses seeks out capable men who trust in God, truthful men who are not covetous, to give them leadership over both small and large groups of the people. When smaller matters arise, these men can judge. Only the largest difficulties shall go to Moses. The leaders, judges over smaller things, Jeh-Jeh tells Moses, "will bear the burden with you, so you will be able to endure, and all these people will also go to their place in peace."

Moses follows Jeh-Jeh's advice. I am very glad. Now he has more time to be with his boys—and with his wife!—instead of being too busy with others' problems all day until he scarcely has time even to eat.

My husband must say goodbye to his father-in-law tomorrow, and Jeh-Jeh will depart for his own land. He will bless us all before he leaves in the morning. It's painful to know he may not see his grandsons, nor his daughter, for a long time; but he will leave in comfort, for he has seen, already, the results of his excellent advice.

Toward Sinai

Camping at Rephidim has been fairly comfortable, but we must move on and find more feed for the livestock. And so we are on our way this morning, moving into the Wilderness of Sinai.

Just three months ago, we left Egypt on the way to the land promised to Abraham. The promise was made by God, Moses says, several hundred years ago, and he is certain God will keep His promise.

Camping in the wilderness is difficult, but the Israelites, all descendants of Abraham, are eager to possess their land. Moses talks to me often about it. Although he is over eighty years old already, he is eager to get to that land he has heard so much about. He says our family shall receive a portion as our own.

I say I'm not an Israelite. How can I go into the land? Moses tells me that because I am the mother of two Israelite males I am accepted as an Israelite. I'm also to partake of the promise!

My heart and my feet want to dance for joy. But dancing must wait. Instead we travel on, following the glowing cloud before us.

As we're treading through the sand and rocks, Moses points to a far-away bush. Very solemnly he tells me that's the bush where God spoke to him from fire. He says it was there God had told him that the very place on which he was standing was holy ground. He was so afraid to look at God, he tells me this afternoon, that he hid his face.

He says that's where he heard God tell him to bring His people out of Egypt. He reminisces, with shame, about arguing with God, insisting God should send someone else, because he didn't think he was the right one to go.

Moses tells me, as we walk farther along in the wilderness, that the Lord wouldn't accept his excuses. Instead He gave him a special sign to prove that the God above all gods had chosen him for the task. The sign, which he tells me, almost in whispers, is that when he had brought the people out of Egypt, he himself would have the privilege to bow and worship the one true God on this very mountain, Mount Sinai. It is the mountain we are nearing.

Moses is so moved he begins to tremble. He sobs softly. Tears trickle into his beard as he shares with me what he is looking forward to, that very sacred meeting on the mountain.

Listening now to Moses, I am seeing his God, as through a mist but each day a bit more clearly—his God, the majestic and holy One. I also am moved to tears. Quietly, I weep with him.

Tonight all tribes of Jacob-Israel spread their campsites before the mountain, exactly the same day of the third month since we left Egypt.

On Mount Sinai

Early this morning, Moses blesses his two sons and me. Then we watch him beginning his climb to meet with God. The Lord calls to him from the mountain, telling him what to say to the Israelites. Since now I feel I truly am an Israelite, God's words are to me as much as to the rest of Jacob's descendants.

This vast basin where we camp at the foot of Sinai possesses amazing acoustics. When we are quiet, we can hear Moses speak even from a long distance away. I slip over as close as possible anyway, not wanting to miss anything God has spoken to Moses.

First God reminds Moses—and the people—of what He did to the Egyptians, and how He brought His people to Himself, like an eagle bears her young on her wings when teaching them to fly.

Then Moses repeats what God says, something so wonderful all the people gasp.

God says if the Israelites obey His voice and keep covenant with Him, they shall be *a special treasure to Him above all other people*, for He chooses them to be a holy nation, a kingdom of priests for Himself. From far into the crowd I hear sounds of awe and excitement.

Moses comes down from the place on the rock where God has spoken this morning, and calls together the elders of the tribes. He tells them all that God has spoken to him. They answer together, "All that the Lord has spoken we will do." Moses brings back their words to God.

Then God tells him to sanctify all the people so they will be ready on the third day, for on that day the Lord will come down on Mount Sinai in the sight of all the people. With his old parents and Miriam, his sister, we consecrate ourselves, body and soul, to the Lord.

It is a fearful thing I'm facing. Moses says God Himself will come down onto Mount Sinai. I'm sure the Lord is absolutely pure and holy. I'm not. What shall I do? God Who hears, what can I do?

After fretful sleep in the night, I wake early, for this is the third day. I hear the growing rumble of thunder. I peep out of the tent and see flashes of lightning. A thick heavy cloud is on the mountain. Inside my heart I feel a deep dread of what this day may bring.

I don't feel like eating, but the boys must have breakfast. I cook manna for them while the thunder grows louder every moment. Then comes a very loud trumpet blast. Everyone in the camp is now awake.

Moses calls for the people to come out of the camp to meet with God. I'm not the only one trembling as we stand near the foot of the mountain. Mount Sinai is covered in smoke, for the Lord has come down on it in fire. The whole mountain shakes violently. We are terrified!

The trumpet's long blast gets longer and increasingly louder. Then Moses speaks, and the Lord answers him by voice, calling him to the top of the mountain. Moses goes up higher and higher until he's swallowed by the cloud and smoke, finally disappearing from my sight.

All around me people are crying in fear. I also am weeping copiously, holding Eliezer tightly in my arms, while Gershom clings to my skirts.

Out from the thick cloud and smoke, Moses comes down to tell the people, again, not to come close to the mountain. God knows that some of them want to break through to see the Lord; but if they do, they will die. So Moses warns them never to dare such a thing.

The people listen carefully when Moses tells us the words which God has spoken. God declares Himself to be their Lord (now mine, too!), the God Who brought them out of their bondage in Egypt.

They must have no other God. They must never make a carved or molded image of any created thing in order to bow down to it or serve it. God alone is God.

They must never use the name of the Lord carelessly or in vain. If they do, the Lord will hold them guilty.

They must remember that the seventh day of each week is to be the Sabbath, a holy day of rest, and no work.

They must honor their fathers and mothers.

They must never murder, never commit adultery, never steal, never give false witness against others, and they must not covet anyone or anything that belongs to someone else.

As we listen, we see the lightning, hear thunder and the blast of the trumpet, and see the mountain smoking. I want to move far away from the mountain.

The leaders call to Moses, "When you speak with us, we will hear; but don't let God speak with us or we may die!"

My heart is pounding furiously. The pounding eases, when Moses says to us all, "Don't fear. God has come to test you, so that you will always honor Him. The fearsome One Who speaks today wants you to know what a powerful God He is, so that you may not sin. He says, 'Don't make for yourselves gods of silver or gold. *I alone am God!*'"

I am so frightened that slowly I keep stepping backwards to be far away. Moses goes farther into the thick darkness where God is. There God gives him very serious words to pass on to the people—words and judgments!

Moses tells us those words and judgments when he comes down. And the people say, with one accord, "All the words which the Lord has said we will do."

Tonight I'm fearful. I said the same words as the other people, but how can I be sure I will always obey God? I don't trust myself, and so I feel afraid. God is beautiful to my soul, and I want never to disappoint Him. *If only God's words could be written on my heart!*

Something Moses told us today seems far above meaningful to me. God had said, "Behold, I send an Angel before you to keep you in the way …" If God's Angel keeps me in His way, I need not fear. Yet I do, for He added, "Beware of Him and obey His voice; do not provoke Him … for My Name is in Him."

Tonight, I want to talk with Moses about my fears, but he has been writing down the full message of the Lord and His judgments. I add more oil to his flickering lamp, and try to sleep.

Midway through the night, I rouse enough to cover Eliezer again. Moses is still bent over with his quill and ink. Even if I dared to peek over his shoulder, I can't read Hebrew. I lie down again to toss—and dream of fire on the mountain.

Moses rises early this morning, and builds an altar at the foot of the mountain, plus twelve pillars according to Israel's twelve tribes. He has twelve young men offer burnt offerings and sacrifice peace offerings of oxen to the Lord. Moses sprinkles half of the blood on the altar, and keeps the other half in basins.

Then, while all the people can hear, he reads the Book of the Covenant. All the people say, "We will do all that God says we should do. We will be obedient." Then Moses takes the basins of blood, sprinkles blood on the people, and announces, "This is the blood of the covenant, which the Lord has made with you according to all these words."

I don't understand. What has the blood to do with the covenant? How can blood confirm the covenant between God and His people? I can't ask Moses what it means, because Moses and his assistant Joshua are starting to go up onto the mountain now.

Moses calls back to the people, "Wait for us. Wait until we come back to you. Both Aaron and Hur are with you. You can go to them if you have difficulties.

Into the Cloud

God calls Moses to go up into the midst of the cloud which has been covering Mount Sinai. To us below, the sight of the glory of God is like a consuming fire on the top of the mountain. Moses goes higher and higher. I strain my eyes to watch as he climbs even higher and seems to be swallowed by the glowing cloud.

I cannot see Moses at all now. He's hidden completely from my sight by the cloud that seems to be afire. When shall I see my precious husband again?

Or shall I?

One week goes by, and then another. My young son wants to be with his father, and wonders why he can't even see him. I try my best to explain that his father is with God on the mountain. He doesn't understand, but seems somewhat comforted by my calm answer.

He and other little boys cleverly make up games to play, sometimes different games each day. I hear their happy laughter from many areas of our camp.

The children are far less troubled than the women who flock around me with multiple questions. I turn their concerns into opportunities for us all to become better acquainted.

I ask them to be my teachers, so that I can understand more about Abraham, and about the Promised Land to which we are going. Then I discover that they are quite ignorant of the history of the Israelites, having been only the weary wives of slaves under Pharaoh's vicious cruelty.

For the younger women, I try to help them sense their freedom. I show them how freeing it could be to dance a bit wildly in the desert sand, swirling silken scarves above their heads. I urge them to picture themselves as princesses on some far-away shore or regal mountain site.

Are they unable to use their imaginations? I know they are fearful about the mountain which seemed to swallow Moses. I tell them Moses is talking with God there. Each day I keep trying to diminish their fears, and encourage them to enjoy the breezes that ruffle their hair. They seem to choose anxiety and gloom instead.

Today I give up, and go back to our tent. Moses' mother Jochabed is old and wrinkled, but shows more life than those young women!

I shouldn't be critical, I suppose. I find it difficult to imagine living as part of a slave's family—for many many years. I shouldn't be shocked that they know little of God, the God with Whom Moses has been on Sinai these many days.

Golden Calf

More days pass, and the people are becoming very anxious and fearful. I hear them ask, "Where is Moses? What has become of this man who brought us out of Egypt?"

After several weeks have gone by, hundreds of people come to Aaron and demand that he make gods to lead them—*gods who cannot hear or speak.*

No! No! Surely this isn't happening! Aaron foolishly yields to their protests. He tells them to bring him all the golden rings from their families' ears. I see him accept great heaps of gold which he molds with an engraving tool until it looks like some sort of calf.

Several people begin to chant, "This is your god, O Israel, the god that brought you out of the land of Egypt!" Aaron makes an altar before it, and proclaims, this evening, that tomorrow is a day of feasting.

This morning I don't want to go out of our tent. I smell burnt offerings and sacrifices. Sounds of revelry get louder and louder. It seems the people are giving themselves to utter debauchery, corrupting not only themselves but also many others around them.

Oh, Israel! How can you? Do you not remember how the one true God brought you out of Egypt with a powerful hand? You promised to obey His commands. Empty promises to God from His people! Moses will be broken-hearted when he sees what I'm seeing as I peep through the tent-flap.

Suddenly *I see Moses!*

He's coming down the mountain! The people are partying so wildly they don't even notice. He descends carefully, with Joshua at his side. He seems to be holding something heavy in his hands. I throw open the tent and run toward the mountain, with Eliezer in my arms and Gershom running behind me.

Somebody shouts, "Here comes Moses!" From one end of the camp to the other I hear the cry repeated, "Here comes Moses! Here comes Moses!"

At once the boisterous crowd begins to quiet down, hastily trying to cover their nakedness—except for those who are so drunk they just wallow on the ground wailing, arms and legs entangled. I try to ignore the scenes near me and keep running toward Moses.

Abruptly I halt! I see fury on his face!

He is hot with anger at the sight of the golden calf, and the wild partying in pagan worship before it. He lifts high above his head the heavy stone tablets in his hands, and throws them hard onto the rocks at the foot of the mountain. They shatter into bits.

He grabs the gold calf they are worshiping, and throws it onto the fire of the altar. The melted gold he grinds into powder, throws it into the water, and makes the people drink it.

Any of the revelers who still had good sense have quickly retreated to their tents, and probably don't hear Aaron's lame excuse for what he had done.

How dare he say what I hear him tell Moses? "Well, you know these people. They are set on evil. They came to me and begged me to make some gods to go before them. They said, 'We don't know what has become of this man Moses who brought us out of Egypt, and we want gods who will lead us.' So I told them to bring their gold earrings, and when I threw them into the fire this calf came out."

Moses is sickened that Aaron didn't restrain the people. He knows such failure will bring great shame to the Israelites when their enemies hear of it. His heart must be aching dreadfully when he stands at the entrance of the camp and shouts, "Whoever is on the Lord's side, come here to me!"

All the men of the Levi tribe gather together before Moses. He tells them, "The Lord God of Israel says to take your swords, and go in and out throughout the camp, and kill … "

I don't hear the rest of it; I hustle our sons into our tent and noisily begin cooking something for our meal. I hear shrieks and wails from many parts of this tent city. Who are the ones being killed? I can easily guess they are the most despicable among the revelers, those who deliberately chose to disobey God's commands, and engaged in what is abominable to Him.

Moses only nibbles at his food this evening, even after forty days and nights on the mountain without food. The happenings of the day have surely taken away his appetite.

Instead he picks up both of his sons, holds them close to his heart, and talks with them. Gershom tells his father, "I was scared when the thunder was so loud and the mountain kept jumping up and down. I was really *really* scared, Mo-mo, when you went into the smoke and fire. But Mommy told me *God* wanted you to go 'way up there and talk with *Him*, and then I stopped being scared."

Moses smiles up at me lovingly. He keeps talking with Gershom, while little Eliezer runs his fingers back and forth through Moses' long white beard, and giggles, with almost a belly-laugh. I smile happily to see the loving threesome.

At last, the boys tire and tumble into bed. Soon Gershom is sound asleep. Eliezer needs milk, and frets instead of sleeping. For him, I bring the nanny goat to our tent door. Finally satisfied, he drifts off to sleep.

Moses' Grief

Late tonight at our special rock, I find Moses weeping, with his head in his hands, his broad shoulders heaving. I lay my hand gently on his arm. He receives me. I sit beside him as he sobs, my tears falling with his.

After a long while, his weeping subsides enough for him to express to me some of his great sorrow. He tells me that, early in his time on the top of Mount Sinai, God had given him commands for the people of Israel, those He has chosen as His special treasure.

For the rest of the forty days and forty nights, God spoke to him things far too wonderful to understand, by such an ordinary human like me. I am in wonder as Moses speaks.

He tells me that the Lord gave him a detailed description of a special Tabernacle for God's worship, to be built while we are at the Sinai camp. God told him what furniture should be made for the Tabernacle, and exactly the size, and shape, and materials, to be used for each piece, and even who should be the major artists and craftsmen in charge of making each item.

Then he begins to sob again. His voice breaking, he says that after God had finished speaking with him, He gave him two tablets of the Testimony, *written by the finger of the Lord on stones God Himself had cut!* Moses had started down the mountain carrying the heavy tablets.

Of course, God Who sees knew what the people had done by making a golden calf, worshiping and sacrificing to it. God Who hears knew they had proclaimed the calf their god who brought them out of the land of Egypt.

But the God of Moses is majestic and holy. He hates unrighteousness and idolatry. Moses says, with sorrow, that God said to him, "I have seen these people, and indeed they are stiff-necked and stubborn. Therefore let Me alone. My wrath will burn hot against them. I will consume them and make of *you* a great nation."

Moses tells me how he, a mere man, had pleaded with the holy and glorious God. "Why should the Egyptians say that You brought them out of Egypt to kill them in the mountains, and rid the earth of them? Please, God! Turn from Your terrible wrath. Remember Your promise to Abraham, and to Isaac and Jacob."

Of course, God had not forgotten as humans do. Yet Moses reminded Him that He had sworn, by Himself, to multiply Abraham's descendants as the stars of heaven. Moses told God, "You promised them a good land which would be their's forever." And the Lord listened to Moses' plea.

Then, he says, he went on down the mountain with the two tablets of stone, each tablet written on both sides, with the writing of God Himself. Those were the tablets he threw down in hot anger, when he saw what a terrible thing the people had done. He smashed them at the foot of Mount Sinai—*precious tablets with God's Own writing!*

He begins to sob again. *He had thrown down the stones God Himself had chiseled, and on which He, the holy One, had written with His Own hand!*

I lay my hand on his shoulder while he weeps. Between sobs, he tells me how he confessed to God His people's great sin of making for themselves a god of gold. He had pleaded for God's forgiveness, and says, softly, that he had asked the Lord to blot *his name* out of the book God had written if He would not forgive the people's terrible sin.

"Moses!" I exclaim. "You asked God to take your name from His book in exchange for all those deplorable sinners?"

He doesn't speak for several minutes. I hear the night-hawk whiz by overhead after a hapless insect. Far away there is the faint yap-yap-yapping of jackals. Otherwise the silence is deep.

At last Moses raises his head. He clears his throat, coughs twice, and continues. He explains that God had said to him, "I will blot out of My book those who sinned against Me; but you, Moses, are to lead My people to the place about which I have spoken to you. I will punish those who have sinned so greatly against Me. They will be blotted out of My book."

Moses tells me that there will be a great plague upon the people as punishment for their wickedness. In the huge camp, I tell him, I observed that the plague had already begun. There will be many graves.

The half-moon shines weakly. Thousands of stars blink overhead. I'd love to stay here on our rock with Moses. I want to share in his grief, and Moses has more to say. Only it must be another night. He is utterly exhausted.

Together we make our way to our tent, and to our mats, Moses almost instantly asleep, his snoring a comfort to me tonight.

The plague has taken a great toll.

After many days, God speaks to Moses, "Leave here, you and the people whom you brought out of the land of Egypt, and go up to the land which I promised to give to Abraham and his descendants. My Angel will go before you and drive out the God-haters and idol-worshipers from the land of Canaan. Go to that very good land."

Moses tells the people what God is saying, and they're in a hurry to pack up and leave for the Promised Land—*tomorrow*. But God has more to say to them, words that make them want to put their hands over their ears instead of listening.

Moses tells them, "God says, 'I Myself will not go up among you. I might consume you on the way, for you are a stubborn and rebellious people.'"

God will not go with them? Dare they go without His Presence? Immediately, the people begin truly to grieve. God tells them to take off all their decorations and jewelry, in mourning. He will decide what to do with them, He says, through His spokesman Moses.

Moses does not know what God will decide. He will wait, perhaps a long time, until God tells him. Moses carries a tent far away from the camp, sets it up there, and calls it the tent or tabernacle of meeting. Anyone who truly humbles himself and desires to seek the Lord God goes to the tent of meeting.

Whenever Moses goes out of the camp to that tent, everybody rises, and all the men stand in their tent doors and watch. When Moses goes inside, the pillar of cloud comes down and rests by the door of the tent. When the people see the pillar of cloud there, every man worships at his own tent door. I detect there are genuine changes taking place in the hearts of these Israelites.

Moses' assistant Joshua remains at the tent of meeting. At evening, Moses comes back to our family tent. He tells me in a hushed voice, filled with awe, that God and he speak *face to face* as good friends.

How wonderful it must be to know God in such a way! Open wide the eyes of my heart, Lord. I want to see You! I must know You, my God!

When he and God spoke face to face in the tent of meeting yesterday, Moses tells me this morning, he had begged God not to make the Israelites go on toward the Promised Land, without His Own Presence with them. As a good friend would do, God listened to Moses' plea, and promised that He Himself will go with him and give him rest.

New Stone Tablets

Today Gershom stops romping with other boys and plops down beside Moses to watch him as he's chiseling two pieces of rock. "Mo-mo," he asks, "what are you making?"

Moses stops chiseling, and gives full attention to his little son. He explains that God told him to make two tablets of stone, like the ones he broke in anger.

He tells Gershom the reason he was angry was that God's people were worshipping a gold calf, instead of the real God, and that God was even more angry than he himself had been.

"But Mo-mo," the young one says, "the people just wanted a god they could see. Why was God so angry about that?"

I listen as Moses explains to Gershom that there is only one God. All pretend gods, which people make out of wood or silver or even gold, can't see or hear or speak or do anything at all. But the real true God can do anything He wants to do.

He asks Gershom if he remembers how God stopped the water at the Red Sea, so we could all go across on dry land.

"Yes, Mo-mo, I remember! I was scared of the soldiers with their chariots, but they couldn't get close to us. The water stood up like a wall, didn't it? I never knew water could do that! Do you think God made it stand up like that?"

Little boys are full of questions, and Moses is happy to help Gershom know the only God. I still have many questions myself, but more and more I am seeing God, through Moses' eyes and heart. God Who hears, I thank You!

Gershom hops up and runs to join the other boys in their play. Moses returns to his work on the stone tablets. He wants each of them to be as smooth as possible.

He tells me that the Lord God ordered him to be ready, on tomorrow's morning, to go up onto Mount Sinai and present himself to Him, on the top of the mountain. No one else may go with him, and no animals dare be herded anywhere near the mountain.

Forty Days and Nights on Sinai

Today there is no thunder or earthquake. Many of the people likely wouldn't even know Moses has gone up, if he hadn't warned them to stay far away from the mountain. It seems God has chosen to descend in the cloud, to meet with Moses in sacred secrecy.

Many days go by. Moses has not returned.

Days, and then weeks, pass, while Moses and God are together on Mount Sinai.

I tremble to think how wonderful it must be, to sit in God's sacred Presence for even a few moments. Surely, later, Moses will tell me what God has said to him there.

More days pass. When will I see Moses again?

Dawn is beautiful this morning, with soft colors only a real God can produce. The colors change to brighter hues as I gaze. And then the sun peeps over the horizon with brilliance I dare not look at. I turn my eyes toward the right and spy a far-away figure descending the mountain.

It's Moses! He has been on the mountain, with God, for forty days and forty nights, and he's coming down now, again holding stone tablets in his hands. In awe, I find myself worshiping the God above all gods.

God has been with Moses, so near that His Own glory is shining now on Moses' face! Moses himself isn't aware that his face is literally aglow with God's glory; but Aaron and all the Israelites see the skin of his face shining, and are very much afraid to go near him.

He calls the elders together, and gives them all the commandments the Lord had spoken to him on the mountain. Also, he tells them about a Tabernacle they are to build for God. When he finishes speaking, he puts a veil over his face.

Whenever he goes into the tent of meeting, to speak with God, he takes the veil off his face; but when he goes out to speak to the people, he covers his face again.

Tabernacle to Be Built

"Whatever are you two up to now?" I ask. I hoist Eliezer onto my hip as I step out of our tent, happy that I've managed to get the child to eat a little manna porridge. Gershom is trotting beside his father on this brilliant sunny afternoon.

Gershom calls back to me, "See that big stone? That's where we began. Mo-mo started with me on his shoulders, but he says I'm getting kinda heavy, so I'm just running to keep up with him. Mo-mo is measuring how long and wide God's Tabernacle will be."

What?

Moses had told me yesterday, his face still shining since he had come down from the mountain, that God had told him to build a Tabernacle where He would live among His people. He says God told him the exact measurements. Late this afternoon he was stepping it off, to get a rough idea of the size.

Building a Tabernacle here in this wilderness? How can that be possible? And when the people of Israel move on to the Promised Land, won't it become a perfect home for someone like Amalek? Surely, that's not what God wants, is it?

I don't ask questions now. Moses is quietly counting as he strides. His smile to me is warm, as he turns sharply to the right, and begins to count again. I'm a bit breathless, trying to keep up with him, while preventing Eliezer from tumbling from my hip. Good thing I inherited bony hips!

Counting is shorter this time. But again he turns right, and begins to count under his breath, a long counting, before a final sharp right turn, which leads to the big stone.

"Here's where we started, Mommy!" Gershom chirps happily. "It will be a big place for God, won't it?"

Yes, I admit it looks very big! Of course, Moses' strides and a carpenter's proper measurements may be considerably different.

Moses smiles happily. "God told me exactly how it should be built, and what size the curtains and each piece of furniture shall be." He says. "I must meet with all the leaders, and give them their instructions, according to each portion for which they are to be responsible. God's dwelling place shall be a beautiful Tabernacle."

I gaze at his face, as he speaks these words to me. Surely, the shining I see must be from the Lord God Himself. No mere human looks like this. Is it possible that God Himself lives inside Moses?

Already leaders from each tribe are gathering near the entrance to the tent of meeting, awaiting instructions from Moses. He will veil his face, as he speaks to them. He says goodbye to us, and Gershom and I watch as he strides away.

I remain puzzled, with dozens of questions. Suddenly, I have a warm wet feeling on the hip that jostles Eliezer. Quickly, I go to our tent to change Eliezer—and myself—with my questions put aside for a few moments. Perhaps Moses' meeting, with all those leaders, will be finished soon enough for him to explain how we can build anything here in this desert.

But my dreams of Moses' early return fail to materialize.

Darkness overtakes us, and hundreds of men remain before Moses. Torches are lit, meal-time is long past, and still they listen intently.

Both boys are asleep. I would be asleep, also, except for my mind's rummaging over and over about a Tabernacle. Bricks need straw mixed with clay soil. No one can make bricks with sand! How then can walls be built?

And Moses had said the Tabernacle would go with us to every camp site. If somehow bricks can be made, how can walls be carried from camp to camp?

I've seen Moses' God do many miracles already—the Red Sea crossing, water from the rock, and lots more. Will He also pick up the building and carry it? Or will the building mysteriously move itself?

Rolling and tossing, sleeping and waking, my mind full of unanswerables—I give up! God Who hears, please let me fall asleep …

It's morning! At my side, Moses rouses himself. The day begins. And soon all my questions are answered. How valuable were my worries!

Moses tells me the Tabernacle will be made with tall boards of acacia wood—more than twice as tall as my Moses! Those boards will be covered with gold, and surrounded by exquisitely embroidered curtains. If I understand what Moses describes, the boards will be held together by gold-covered rods, passing through gold rings. The curtains will also, somehow, be linked with each other.

A builder I'm not. I don't understand how it will be put together—nor how it can be moved from one camp site to the next. I tell myself that I really don't need to understand. My curiosity must not overcome my good sense. And my good sense tells me God has described to Moses exactly how to do what God has told him should be done, or God wouldn't have told him about the Tabernacle in the first place!

My heart wishes I could help make something for the place where God says He will live among His people. But what can I do?

Just when I am beginning to feel quite unnecessary, Moses says that because I have skills both for spinning and for embroidering, I will have a part in making the large and very beautiful curtains for God's dwelling. With joy, I thank You, God!

Today, in every tribe, the leaders are amassing gold and silver jewelry, onyx, precious gem-stones, blue and purple and scarlet thread, and more—free-will offerings of the people.

All day long, the offerings keep coming, from earrings and nose rings, bracelets, necklaces, brooches, silver and bronze objects, and much more—above what is needed for the work, until Moses gives the command to bring no more.

Obviously, hearts are stirred to give for the work of the Lord's Tabernacle, and for elaborate garments of the priests who will serve God there. Everyone seems to bubble over with joy—true joy, not at all like their previous pagan frivolity. I perceive it as sacred and holy excitement. I feel it, too.

Now the sun is setting. Tomorrow is the Sabbath, when no one shall work. It will be a time of rejoicing for the goodness of the Lord.

Watching the Builders

While Eliezer and Jochabed nap this afternoon, Moses takes me with him. We walk around the camps, and watch the people hard at work at all sorts of projects necessary for the Lord's Tabernacle.

"How can they make everything just as God told you it should be made?" I ask. "Surely there has to be a very special superintendent, for such a massive work."

Moses says there is such a superintendent. His name is Bezalel, grandson of Hur, of the tribe of Judah.

"Bezalel?" I ask. "Isn't he just another man, like many thousands around us? How can he get the work done, in precisely the way God wants it done?"

Moses explains that God had called Bezalel, *by name*, to do the work. He adds, "The Lord has filled him with the Spirit of God, in wisdom and understanding, and in knowledge of all manner of workmanship. God has given him the ability to design artistic works."

He goes into more detail, saying Bezalel can work in gold and silver and bronze, and even in cutting jewels for setting, as well as in carving wood.

Impatiently I interrupt. (Impatience and interrupting and are two things I'm good at, I admit.) "But he can't possibly do everything himself! Besides, I see everybody around him making things only artists ... "

This time Moses interrupts me. "God has also given him the ability to teach—both to him and to his major assistant Aholiab from the tribe of Dan—besides the skill to weave and embroider."

Moses goes on, "The curtains shall have artistic designs of cherubim ... "

I see many heavy curtains being made, curtains woven of fine linen, and with blue and purple and scarlet thread.

I say, with humbling second thoughts, "And I had thought I was doing something special by spinning goat hair."

Moses chuckles and squeezes my hand. "You and the other gifted women are providing the blue, purple, and scarlet yarn and fine linen, without which the necessary curtains can't be made," he says. "God has filled your hearts with wisdom, for doing truly essential work."

I am humbled to think I'm spinning yarn for God's sanctuary, *to honor Him*! I see that God can be pleased by what seems my very small gift. I begin to understand that nothing is small in His sight, if done *from the heart,* for Him.

I had wondered, as we prepared to leave Egypt, why Moses had carefully wrapped many rolls of parchment and tucked them away in our cart. Now I know he had needed many sheets of that parchment, on which to write every word which God had spoken to him on the mountain, words of commandments and of covenant for the Israelites.

Also, on sheets of parchment, he probably sketched the furniture which shall go inside the holy Tabernacle. Bezalel and the other workers must have patterns, so that every piece is made exactly as God had shown Moses.

I'm musing about this when Moses says, "We've walked enough around the work stations for today," and we turn toward our own tent. "Perhaps, in a few more days, you may go with me near the edges of the stations, where the Tabernacle furniture is being made."

He adds, "The entire Tabernacle is holy for the Lord, but the furniture for the inside is too holy for us to approach. Consecrate yourself for a distant view, my dear little wife."

I gaze at his face as he speaks. That precious face shines. What a wonderful God is He with Whom my husband speaks—face to face! How would He deign to come and live among us, in the Tabernacle we *very human* people are building?

A wondrous surprise awaits our return to our temporary desert home.

Jochabed and Amram and Moses' elder sister Miriam occupy one side of our large tent. A flap between can be raised or lowered as needed. Today, the flap is raised. Jochabed is cuddling Eliezer, and smiling broadly as we arrive.

"Moses!" Jochabed calls. "Watch!" She stands Eliezer to his feet, and tells Moses to hold out his arms toward his son. Eliezer takes three tentative steps, tumbles, gets up, and takes two more steps, grinning gleefully as he falls into Moses' arms. Our little one's very first steps!

Somehow, Tabernacle-building takes second place at this moment.

Sacred Furniture

For a little while this afternoon, after our noon meal, and with Eliezer settled down for a nap beside his grandpa Amram, Moses and I walk quickly near the working spaces where craftsmen are building the Tabernacle furniture.

Moses explains a little about each item on which the crews are working. On a large flat rock to our left, someone is hammering gold into what I think looks like an enormous lampstand. Moses says I'm right. It is a lampstand, with three branches on each side of a wide and strong center shaft.

Not far from that work station, workers are building something Moses says is the incense altar. It will be covered completely with gold, he says. It will be used to offer incense for God.

"What kind of incense?" I'm full of questions, as usual.

Moses says that God Himself has given the recipe for special incense, to be burned only for Him. No one must dare to make it or use it for themselves.

In the distance, workers are covering, with gold, the table for the bread of the Presence. And still farther away I see something like a long box. It's also being covered, both inside and outside, with gold.

In a soft voice Moses says, "That's the Ark of the Covenant." He tells me that the stones on which God has written will be put into the Ark, as will also a container of manna.

I ask quietly, "Why does God want those in the Tabernacle?"

"The manna," says Moses, "is for remembrance of God's miraculous provision for His people. The tablets of stone are those on which God expressed His covenant with His people, and wrote His commandments. They warn of God's judgment upon anyone who does not obey the Holy One."

I remember the plague which killed many thousands who disobeyed. "Is there no place for forgiveness?" I wonder aloud, and Moses points to a very far-away workplace where gifted artists are beating gold into what looks like—well, like cherubim, with great wings …

Moses whispers, "There is the Mercy Seat, the cover of the Ark."

Is this feeling in my heart a holy reverence? Or is it just wonder at the beauty of the workmanship? Lord God Who hears, who am I in Your Presence just now? Can I ever be holy enough to approach You? Please change me, in whatever way You choose, and make me one of Your very Own.

Only God can hear what my heart is saying, and I know He hears!

Moses says we must go no closer to the holy furniture of the Tabernacle. We turn back towards our tent, but my heart wants to stay near. Somehow, I feel I am truly worshiping God as I go.

Interlude

I take Eliezer for a walk. Oh, no! He takes *me* for a walk! He refuses to be carried. He exults in his new-found freedom from crawling around like a desert turtle. And is he curious! He's interested in every little thing. He stops to watch a caterpillar crawl, and then a line of ants marching, until they disappear under a rock.

He tumbles often, but pays little attention to his scraped knees. The wide world is his at last!

When he tires, and we return home, I tell Moses about our escapade. He says, "Eliezer is very much like his mother! He even has hair as dark as yours. And his eyes twinkle like yours, with a little bit of mischief showing, too." He tosses his wee child into the air a few times, while they both laugh in delight.

When Eliezer begins to yawn and rub his eyes, it's time for his midday nap. I lay him down beside Amram. Soon they are both asleep.

Then I walk over to the teaching place. There Gershom is learning to read and to write Hebrew. How I would like to join the learners so that I also can read Hebrew! But this learning is, for some reason, not for females. Still I can catch some of what the leaders are telling the young fellows about their ancestry.

Old men of the Issachar tribe are fervently helping younger Israelite males to know the history of Israel, lest they fail to appreciate from whence they have sprung. Moses himself has told Gershom about God's relationship with Abraham, and with Isaac and Jacob, and I have learned much as I listened.

I'm grateful that these young males, at the teaching place, have an opportunity to gain extensive knowledge of their long history. Surely, they will choose to honor the God who promised Abraham the land to which we are going, *the Promised Land!*

The students, some already twelve or older, and others as young as Gershom, eagerly soak up the stories of their history. Again, I listen from the outskirts of the crowd gathered today. It seems God has gifted Issachar's tribe with teaching ability, and I'm grateful. (I'm still wistful for a small space of my own among the learners!)

Dear Father Amram had been badly injured by Pharaoh's cruel slave-drivers. Now, in old age, he can scarcely stand or take even two steps. He has a great longing to see the Tabernacle being built, and so, each evening, Moses honors him by describing, as the work progresses, the many large ornate curtains and every piece of furniture—and describing it so thoroughly that his father can almost feel himself observing the work.

This evening, Moses paints a word-picture of the lamp, which will stand near the wall in the south side of the holy place. He tells Father Amram that the lampstand is like a very sturdy stem with six branches. "There are three branches on the right side and three on the left," Moses says, "and the entire lamp is made of pure hammered gold, in one piece."

"How can it be?" wonders Father Amram. I also wonder. I keep listening as Moses describes the six lamp cups shaped like almond blossoms, with their buds and petals. "Even the stem has hammered gold almond blossoms, Father," says Moses. "God gave His Spirit to the craftsman who has done this work. No one could have done such magnificent work, without God working through him."

Amram is satisfied with Moses' explanation. He says, "I have been young. Now I am old. I want to go into the Promised Land before I die. But if I may not, I shall be content to see the Tabernacle God's people are building for His dwelling."

My father-in-law is too tired to listen longer. Moses bends down to kiss him on each cheek and quietly leaves the tent.

Whenever I have opportunity to watch the curtain makers and embroiderers, or the furniture builders, I never see anyone seeming to be in a hurry. And yet all the work in progress meets Moses' approval, for quality and timeliness. Very soon the priests' clothing will be complete, and the Tabernacle will be finished and set up, readied for worship.

Priests' Garments

As the high priest, Aaron's garments will be far more beautiful and regal than anything I've ever seen. Moses tells me gold threads are being cut from very thin sheets of beaten gold, and those gold threads are worked together with blue, purple, and scarlet, in artistic designs, woven in fine linen for Aaron's ephod. On the hem of the blue robe of the ephod are to be pomegranates interspersed with bells of pure gold.

God is interested in the finest details, Moses says. Aaron and his four sons are to wear tunics, turbans, sashes, and short trousers, all woven of fine linen.

"Why trousers?" I ask, in surprise. "They're to wear robes, aren't they? So why trousers, too?"

Moses chuckles at my question. Then he explains that the bronze altar for burnt sacrifice has stairs to approach the fire pit. God wants the priests' nakedness to be carefully covered, when they do their work at the altar.

Abruptly, he changes the subject. "Zipporah, do you know why the workers asked the women to give their bronze mirrors? The priest must have a laver in which to wash, after burning the sacrifice, before he enters the sanctuary. The laver will be covered entirely with bronze. And you helped, dear one, by giving your mirror for the Lord's work."

"Moses," I say, embarrassed, "I kept my smallest mirror so I can try to look nice for you."

Moses chuckles again, and squeezes my hand.

I'm glad that my part, in the Tabernacle and worship, is more than spinning goat hair and doing some embroidery. I'm glad I could honor God with each little part.

But I had interrupted Moses again, as he was giving the description of the rest of the high priest's garments, for wearing in the Holy Place.

Moses says that on each shoulder of the ephod will be an onyx stone in a setting of gold, each stone engraved with names of the sons of Jacob-Israel. "The high priest will carry on his shoulders the children of Israel, when he enters the Holy Place," Moses says, "and also over his heart, in a breastplate with twelve precious gems set in gold, each one engraved with the name of one of the tribes of Israel."

"Those gems must be from some the Egyptians gave us as we were preparing to leave Egypt," I say. "Do you remember which ones will be on the breastplate?" Moses says that among them are emerald, sapphire, sardius, beryl, lapis lazuli, turquoise, topaz ... "

"Ooh!" I exclaim. "Lapis and turquoise are my favorites! But twelve gems, all set in gold, must make it very heavy for the high priest who wears it on his chest," I say, and Moses agrees.

"Do you think the weighty breastplate is a symbol of Israel's being heavy on God's heart?" I ask. Moses nods soberly.

I know that God has chosen Israel, out of all peoples, to be His special treasure. But they're often stubborn and rebellious. Surely His heart is heavy because of them. Moses himself has experienced effects of their disdain for holiness. He grieves with God!

Moses finishes his description of the priests' garments, holy garments, which are to be worn only when the priests are serving at the Tabernacle. He says the Lord told him the priest will wear a turban, with a crown of pure gold. On that crown will be this inscription, like the engraving of a signet: *HOLINESS TO THE LORD*. It will be tied to a blue cord and fastened above the turban.

Today, Moses inspects every item which God commanded to be made for the Tabernacle. He is satisfied that each thing is done according to God's pattern, as shown him on the mountain. All the beautiful work is finished!

Now men, with long brushes from trees or bushes, are making the ground ready for the Tabernacle, being sure that not even a small stone will be left.

Tonight, Moses tells me that on the morrow—the first day of the first month of the second year since we left Egypt—the Tabernacle will be set up. The joy we face tomorrow makes sleeping tonight nearly impossible!

Tabernacle Erected

Somehow, I slept a little. Moses is up early, already instructing the assigned workers exactly where to place the sockets of silver into which the boards are to be set.

Dear old Father Amram weeps, because his legs cannot carry him to observe the erection of the Tabernacle. I see his grief, and so I make a padded seat for him, in the cart, and beg two strong young men to carry him and gently seat him there.

I guide our faithful donkey, as he pulls the cart a little closer to the Tabernacle site. Eliezer is safe in the cart beside his grandfather.

I see no other women in the vast crowd. Probably, to the many thousands of men, I also am quite invisible.

Amram weeps again, but this time his tears are for joy, when he sees the gold-covered boards put into their sockets. He raises his hands in praise to the great God of heaven, his joyous shout as powerful as his fainting heart allows.

When the boards are in place with their bars, and the pillars are raised up, the curtains are spread out over the Tabernacle, with their covering on top, as the Lord had commanded Moses.

Then Moses reverently carries the tablets of the Testimony and places them into the Ark. With great care he sets the Mercy-Seat on top of the Ark, the pure gold cherubim hovering over it with wings outstretched.

Standing by the donkey's nose, with Gershom beside me, I crane my neck, but because of so many others crowding around to watch, I miss seeing the Ark brought into the Tabernacle.

How is that precious Ark, with the Mercy-Seat covering it, and the cherubim spreading their wings over it, carried into the Most Holy Place? Is my Moses, strong as he is, able to do it himself? Dare it be touched by other human hands?

Somehow, the Ark has been placed within the Most Holy Place. Now I can see the high and heavy curtain-veil being hung on its four poles.

God had told Moses exactly where to place the veil. It will completely partition the Most Holy Place, with its Ark of the Testimony, from the larger part of the Tabernacle, the Holy Place. The high priest alone is allowed to enter the Most Holy Place, and that only once a year. No one else may even see the Ark and the Mercy-Seat.

Outside the veil, by the north wall of the Tabernacle's Holy Place, the gold-covered table of the bread of the Presence will be situated, and the bread set in order on it, before the Lord. I catch a glimpse of the table being carried in.

Other gawkers block my sight when the lamp of the Holy Place is placed, at the south side of the Tabernacle.

The last item is the golden altar of incense at its place in front of the veil. Moses had explained that altar to me. I cannot see the incense altar carried into its place, but I take a deep breath and imagine I can smell the sweet incense to be burned on it for the Lord.

Then the screen curtain is hung up at the door of the Tabernacle.

I'm unable to see the large altar for burnt sacrifice, but I know that between that altar and the Tabernacle entrance is the laver, covered with bronze, for which we women have given our mirrors. Moses told me Aaron and his sons are to be washed at that laver.

Then Aaron will be clothed with the high priest's garments and the four sons with their tunics.

Now the courtyard all around the Tabernacle is carefully raised up, with the screen at the entrance gate.

With Amram and Jochabed, I am among the great multitude watching with bated breath, as Moses finishes the work, exactly as God commanded. When all is in place, Moses does as he has been instructed by the Lord: he anoints the Tabernacle and all that is in it, to consecrate it and make it holy.

Next he anoints the altar of burnt offering and all its utensils, and consecrates the altar as most holy for the Lord. Then Aaron and his sons are anointed, and set apart as holy servants for the Lord's work.

We are only spectators; still we are in awe as the beautiful Tabernacle for God is completed and raised up.

But nothing has prepared us for the glory which we see now! When Moses finishes anointing each article, as well as Aaron and his four sons, according to God's command, the sacred cloud moves down and envelopes the Tabernacle of meeting.

Then God Himself fills the Tabernacle with His glory.

Moses is not able to enter—the glory is far too great *even for him who speaks face to face with God!*

Dear Father Amram is prostrate on the cart floor, overcome by what his eyes have seen. I'd like to linger with the other Israelites, as they worship the One and Only God, the One Who has promised to be with us, as we travel to the Promised Land.

Instead, I maneuver the cart around worshipers, and turn it towards our tent, to care for Amram.

As we help him into the tent, he is more feeble than I have ever seen him. But his smile is beautiful! He seems full of a wonderful peace. He says, in a voice little more than a whisper, "I have seen His glory. Now I am satisfied to be gathered to my fathers."

He sags to his knees, and slumps down, his eyes slowly closing, but his smile remaining. Jochabed kisses his withered cheek. There is no response. With her hair she wipes her tears away.

How can I explain to Eliezer why he cannot nestle to sleep in the crook of Grandpa Amram's arm? Surely, he didn't understand when two Levite men gently wrapped his grandfather's empty shell in a shroud, and carried it away to a grave dug near the foot of Mount Sinai. He is a very puzzled little boy, and looks all around for the missing one. Finally, he begins to cry. I hold him and cry with him.

Moses says his father had always worshiped the God of Abraham. Now he has seen the glory of the One Whom his soul loved more than life itself. He was one-hundred-thirty-seven years old. For all his life, Moses says, he truly believed and followed God. He had been an outstanding example to men of the tribe of Levi.

Moses doesn't say it, but certainly Amram had great influence on his own life. True, Moses was adopted as the son of Pharaoh's daughter, but he never forgot his roots. Often he came for a few days, Jochabed tells me, to sit at his father's feet and soak up knowledge he could not have gotten elsewhere.

Living in two very disparate worlds, Moses turned his heart to the God of Abraham. God was at work preparing him to know and to worship the true God, and to lead his people from the worship of Egypt's many idols to see the glory of God Himself. How grateful I am to have been a participant in this spiritual journey!

Israel Worships

Aaron and his sons have been commanded by the Lord, to stay at the door of the Tabernacle, day and night, for seven days after Moses has anointed them. These seven days are to complete their consecration.

On the eighth day, Moses calls Aaron and his sons, along with the elders of Israel, and gives them instructions concerning offerings to the Lord.

The offerings God desires are not like offerings my father, and others in our compound, had offered to our gods. Those gods couldn't hear or speak or do anything except just stand there. They couldn't eat the food we placed solemnly before them. When I was a child I used to wonder how the food disappeared overnight, but I simply accepted the deception, however it happened.

Our gods bore no resemblance to One Whom I now know is the true God, the God of Abraham and of the Israelites. Offerings to Him are precisely defined by the One Who is worshiped. There must be burnt offerings to make atonement for the sins of the priests, and of the common people, and other sacrifices and offerings.

On this day, each animal for burnt sacrifice has been brought to the altar, slain there, and the blood poured or sprinkled around the altar. Then Aaron lifts his hand toward the people, blesses them, and comes down from the altar.

Although I am far back in the crowd, I am able to see Aaron and Moses go into the Tabernacle. I suppose Moses needs to explain carefully to Aaron how God wants him to carry out his high-priestly duties.

When they come back out, they bless the people again. God's glory appears to all of us when sudden fire comes out from the Lord, and consumes the burnt offering already burning on the altar. All of us shout with loud voices and fall with our faces to the ground, before the great God of all the earth.

I am so thrilled I'm in tears, which makes mud on my face, of course. Eliezer tries, unsuccessfully, to clean my face when I rise. I hug him, and cry some more.

What a blessed time we have experienced here before Mount Sinai—a marvelous day of great joy and celebration for all the Israelites!

But tonight, Moses tells me of a terrible thing that happened today!

He says two of Aaron's sons, Nadab and Abihu, burned incense, which God had not ordered them to do. Evidently, they lightly esteemed God's holiness, and fire from the Lord destroyed them.

"But they had been anointed to be priests!" I exclaim, horrified. "Why would God kill anyone already anointed to serve Him as a priest?"

Moses says God has declared that whoever comes near Him must regard Him as holy, so that He will receive the glory He deserves, before all the people.

"God must not be carelessly treated as someone only a little higher than a human being. We must not think that He is just *The Big Man in The Cloud*," Moses says. "He is holy, and He wants all His people to be holy, to bring Him glory."

"But how can we be holy?" I ask. "Maybe I'm only making excuses, but I'm human and faulty. And I'm sure I'm not the only one. Anything that dishonors God is sin, isn't it? Still we *choose* sin which dishonors Him."

Moses tries to say something, but I go on, beginning to weep. "I know I have sinned and disobeyed Him at times. Is there some way to take away my sin, so that I can be holy? I really want to please Him!"

Moses puts his strong arm around my trembling shoulders, and pulls me closer to himself as he speaks. "The sin offering, a lamb of the sheep or goats without a blemish of any kind, was presented to the Lord today. Aaron killed a sin offering for himself, and for the congregation, and sprinkled the blood around the altar."

Again I interrupt, "But why did an innocent lamb have to die?" And Moses responds with another question, "Do you think each person who has sinned should have died today? God says that the soul who sins will die."

"Oh, Moses!" I exclaim. "Then everyone of us should have died!"

"Because He loves us, the Lord allowed an unblemished substitute to die instead," Moses explains gently. "If you had been there, you would have seen Aaron put his hand on the creature's head, as a symbol that he transferred his sin to that perfect animal, who took the sinner's place. A perfect lamb shed its blood for the sinner."

Moses says that God demands shedding of blood for the remission of sin. I don't understand. All this talk about blood-shedding confuses me. How can the Israelites be comfortable with the idea of killing an innocent animal and draining its blood? Why does God only accept blood before He will forgive sin?

I listen, but it seems too much for me. How dare I, who have sinned, let a perfect lamb die in my place? I am humbled greatly to think God may love me so much!

I look toward the Tabernacle and see the fiery cloud covering it. And I bow my heart and worship.

Moving Day

As Moses is leaving our nest at daybreak this morning, he tells me he must call together the elders and leaders of each tribe to tell them all tribes must move to designated places before Passover.

"Why must we move?" I ask, and he calls back, "To prepare for our journey from Sinai to the Promised Land."

His answer doesn't satisfy me, but he is gone before I can ask more. Soon from the Tabernacle entrance comes a long blast on the shofar.

At Moses' signal, elders and leaders quickly gather. He tells them we must leave our current spaces before the fourteenth day of the month, move tents and belongings, and camp in prescribed locations as he directs.

Here we've settled fairly comfortably for many months. When Moses comes back, I ask again, "Why must we move?"

He tells me what he told the leaders—that our move and reorganization is in preparation for the time of departure from Sinai for the Promised Land. Now I understand, and so also do the leaders and elders. But many people are upset and irritated, grumbling about Moses' order.

Even as they complain, they scramble to pack up quickly so as to get the best spots for pitching their tents. There are many noisy arguments and ugly disagreements, with children crying and adding to the din and bedlam.

Suddenly I'm reminded of something from what seems like a long-ago day, when my sisters and I were herding sheep.

One hot afternoon, I spied a gigantic ant-hill and poked a stick into it just to see what would happen. Immediately thousands of ants began racing out, frenzied and disorganized, running helter-skelter, bumping into one another, some carrying food with no place to go, some fighting for space with other ants, all acting very un-antlike, in complete disarray.

I was feeling sorry that I'd disturbed them, until I felt a burning sting on my ankle, and another, and then another on my leg. I ran and never tried that again!

Unlike a swarm of ants in feverish disorder, changing our camp sites has a definite and reasonable purpose, which, however, doesn't make the task any easier at the moment.

I find it exhausting to move our belongings, while keeping Eliezer from wandering off and getting lost in the crowds. His rambunctiousness makes me anxious. When he disappears for a few seconds, panic helps me find him. Jochabed ties him to her sash, despite his yelps and his struggles to be free.

Of course, Moses cannot help. He must be camp-master each day, until everyone is settled. Camping—and marching—arrangements are meticulously designed.

Each tribe is assigned its position around the Tabernacle. Staking their tents in the east is Judah, with the largest number of men old enough to fight in case of attack. When our march is to begin, Judah will lead, with Issachar and Zebulon joining. Such a huge group of well-armed men should be enough to strike fear into all enemies.

On the west are Benjamin, Manasseh, and Ephraim. Dan, Asher, and Naphtali flank the northern side, and Gad, Simeon, and Reuben are on the south.

The Gershonites, Kohathites, and Merarites, descendants of the three sons of Levi who came with Jacob to Egypt, will have charge of the Tabernacle itself, and their camps are nearest the sanctuary.

In spite of all the grumblings and complaints, the moving and setting up at each new camp site has been done with much more order than I first anticipated. And as far as I know, no children were misplaced! Maybe Eliezer wasn't the only one tied to his grandma's apron strings.

When I had heard much arguing from those jostling for the best positions in the new sites, I thought surely God must feel sad. We are all His people, are we not? Dare we selfishly want the highest place? And yet I found myself longing to be somewhere close to Moses' headquarters.

Aaron's two remaining sons, Ithamar and Abiathar, set up their tents east of the Tabernacle entrance. Aaron and Moses already have tents set up there. Of course Joshua's tent will be near Moses' own.

The assigned site for the Kohathites is at the southern side of the Tabernacle. Gershom and Eliezer and I pitch our tent near the east end of the Kohathites' site. We'll be fairly close to Moses' tent. Jochabed is with us, of course, but Miriam chooses, instead, to be near the center of the Levite camp.

Actually I'm relieved. Miriam always seems uncomfortable with me. Perhaps that's because my skin is darker than hers. Or maybe there's more to the issue. Once she chided me for being disrespectful in allowing Gershom to call Moses *Mo-mo*. My own father became *Jeh-Jeh* when I was a tiny child, because my tongue couldn't pronounce the "th" sound in Jethro. Both fathers have said they find the nicknames endearing. I don't know why it should trouble Miriam anyway.

But I've more important things to think about. My little head today is puzzling over how it is possible to move the sacred Tabernacle as we travel on to the Promised Land. I must ask Moses about it.

Moses tells me the descendants of Kohath, the second son of Levi, will be given very specific regulations for transporting every part of the Tabernacle. (Levi's first son was Gershon, and the third was Merari.)

"May I know just a little of those regulations?" I ask. "Maybe it will help me picture what seems totally impossible."

Moses tries to explain briefly. Eliezer naps, but Gershom darts in and out of the conversation. Moses loves this eager boy and patiently tries to answer his questions.

"Several of the tribes have provided the Gershonites and Merarites with wagons in which to carry the boards and bars of the walls, and all the curtains and cords," Moses says. "Of course it takes oxen to pull the wagons, and some tribes are giving oxen for that very use."

Gershom bursts in. "May I help drive the oxen, Mo-mo?" Moses chuckles, and ruffles up Gershom's hair, while he says, "We don't have any oxen to drive, my boy. Other men are already assigned to do that. But thanks for the offer!"

I keep listening as Moses tries to describe traveling days, but I have an urgent question. "Moses," I plead, "please tell me how the holiest things are to be moved from where they are now to another camping place."

Again Gershom breaks in with a question. "When are we going to move?"

Moses answers Gershom first. "When God lifts the cloud off the Tabernacle, we'll move. When the cloud rests, so also will we."

"Oh!" Gershom says. "That's the way God will tell us, right?" Moses nods, and Gershom trots off to play with other boys, while Moses and I continue our conversation.

"The most sacred objects of the Tabernacle will be cared for by the Kohathites themselves," Moses tells me. (Moses and Aaron and his sons are descendants of Kohath. Why God would have chosen the middle son of Levi to be caretaker of the holiest items, instead of choosing the firstborn, only God Himself knows.)

"How will they take care of those holy things?" I ask. "Especially the Ark of the Covenant—they dare not even look at it! How can the Arc and Mercy-Seat accompany the Israelites on our journey?"

"You've asked a good question," Moses says, and answers soberly. "God says Aaron and his sons are to go into the Holy Place, take down the curtain-veil between the Holy Place and the Most Holy Place, and cover the Ark and its Mercy-Seat with that curtain. Over that shall be a special covering of skins, and then, spread over that, another covering entirely of blue."

I ask, "Then the gold-covered poles will be inserted?"

"Yes," says Moses, his voice becoming softer as he speaks. "The dwelling place for God—the Ark with the Mercy-Seat—must be handled with true reverence and awe. The Kohathites are to carry the Ark by the poles on their shoulders. The poles in their rings prevent human hands from touching the Ark."

"And dying!" I exclaim. "How wise is Israel's God—and how compassionate!"

Then, quietly, I ask, "What about the other furniture in the Tabernacle?"

I'm remembering the day when Moses and I walked near the work places, where the holy things were being built. There I had seen poles of acacia wood being overlaid with gold.

"Why are all those poles being very precisely made?" I had asked Moses. He told me they were to be inserted through gold rings at each of the four corners of the Ark of the Covenant, and also of the incense altar and the table of showbread. The Kohathites are to carry each piece with the poles on their shoulders.

As I listen to Moses, my shoulders begin to ache. I mentally picture the Kohathites carrying those things. "God must have chosen very strong men," I say, and Moses agrees.

"The Levites have been especially dedicated by God for every service concerning the Tabernacle," Moses tells me. "They shall begin serving at age twenty-five, and cease when they reach fifty years old."

"After they turn fifty, they just sit and twiddle their thumbs, I suppose," I say flippantly. Moses chuckles and shakes his head. He says, "After they retire, they may assist the working Levites as guards of the Tabernacle, but they will not officiate in any of the service."

How intricately God has designed every part of this place of His dwelling among us! I am humbled to think that He is such a glorious God and yet deigns to love us.

I sit a moment in silence, and then I ask quietly, "What about the golden lampstand? There are no poles for that magnificent piece."

As Moses answers my question, and more, I can picture the golden lampstand with its utensils and containers of oil, put on a *carrying frame,* and covered with a blue cloth.

The incense altar must be similarly covered, and so must the table of showbread with all its bowls and pans and utensils. Then their poles are to be inserted.

Moses says that when Aaron and his sons have finished packing and covering each item, specially designated sons of Kohath may go inside to pick up and carry the units to our next camping site.

"Aaron and his sons shall go in with them," Moses says, "and show them which item each one is to carry. They must wait until they are called. If they go into the Tabernacle, before their proper time, and see any of the holy items, they shall die."

I sit speechless for a few moments, and then I dare to ask, "Who will be the person in charge of those who carry these holy things?" What Moses describes requires holiness of heart, surely. That's far more important than just strength for physical labor.

"The supervision for everything in the entire Tabernacle will be the responsibility of Aaron's son Eleazar," Moses says.

He explains more. "When our journey begins, the Gershonites and Merarites are to take down the Tabernacle. Then the Kohathites shall come and carry the sacred furniture—only by their poles or by carrying frames. With their hands they dare not touch any of the holy things, as you know."

Moses tells me the Gershonites and the Merarites are the load-bearers of the Tabernacle itself, and also of the courtyard around it. They'll make good use of the six wagons and twelve oxen.

"The Gershonites and the Merarites will transport the entire Tabernacle," Moses says. "When the cloud rests, they will set up the Tabernacle, in preparation for the arrival of the Kohathites with the holy furniture."

"What about the altar and the laver?" I ask suddenly. "My mirror has had a part in the laver!" And as soon as those words come off my tongue I feel terribly ashamed. How dare I be so self-centered? How can God love someone like me?

In a hushed voice, Moses says, "The altar and laver have been anointed and sanctified and are holy. The Kohathites will bear all the holy furniture, including the altar, on their shoulders."

"The altar?" I gasp. "It's so big! It must be as heavy as a pile of rocks! Who has shoulders strong enough for … "

Moses interrupts me. "The altar is hollow," he says. "It's made of planks covered with bronze, and the grating is bronze, too. It is not too heavy to be carried on the Kohathites' shoulders."

"Oh!" I say meekly, and Moses continues. "Before we travel, the ashes will be removed. Then the altar is to be covered with a purple cloth. All the equipment used will be put on that cloth and then covered with goatskin leather. The carrying poles will be inserted, ready for the priests to assign the carriers."

"The Kohathites must be strong holy men of God," I exclaim. "Surely the Lord God shall bless every step they take!"

I find myself in uncharacteristic silence on this quiet Sabbath day.

Passover Time

How fast time flies! Already it has been over a year since we left Egypt on our way to the Promised Land. This is the first month of the second year, the fourteenth day—the day in which we shall celebrate Passover.

With Gershom at his side, Moses has selected a lamb without blemish for the Passover sacrifice. Gershom hops up and down with excitement. He wants to tell the story of the first Passover, and Moses happily consents.

"God told His people to kill a perfect lamb," Gershom begins, "and put some of the blood on the sides of the door and over the top. Mo-mo lifted me up high, and I wiped the blood over the door with hyssop leaves. And then at midnight God's angel came to Egypt and passed over all the houses with blood over the doors. All the oldest sons of every family in Egypt died that night if they didn't have blood over the door. I'm the oldest son of this family, but I didn't die, because God's angel saw the blood over our door and passed over us. I'm glad I didn't die that night."

With tears in his eyes Moses tells Gershom, "I'm glad, too, my son." I wipe away tears and see Jochabed doing the same.

At twilight Moses kills the lamb. We roast all of it, not breaking any bones, and eat it with unleavened bread and bitter herbs. What we cannot eat we'll burn in the embers before we go to our beds.

God had told Moses that His people should celebrate Passover every year for all generations. Part of the celebration ought to be telling the story, as little Gershom did tonight.

When Israelites are in the Promised Land, I think telling Israel's story will be very important, lest God's perfect plans for them are forgotten, and God is no longer precious to them. They must not forget the One to Whom they owe the land.

I dare not, even though I'm only a grafted-in Israelite, become careless about the long (and turbulent) history of Jacob-Israel. I want Gershom and Eliezer to know well the stories of Abraham and Isaac and Jacob, so that they can pass them along to generations following.

God Who speaks had told Moses that He had chosen Israel to be His very special treasure. I wonder—when we arrive in the Promised Land, if God's words are forgotten or ignored, what then? God Who hears, will You no longer dwell among Your people as You do now in Your Tabernacle?

I gaze long at the cloud over the Tabernacle, the cloud which gleams with fire all during the night, the cloud which speaks visibly of God's Presence.

And my heart worships.

Toward the Promised Land

As day is breaking, the priests blow the silver trumpets.
Today is the twentieth day of the second month in the second year since we left Egypt. We had just settled into our designated camp-sites before Passover. Can it be possible that we're already beginning our journey?

The Lord has lifted the cloud from the Tabernacle! We gather the day's manna, eat quickly, and begin taking down the tent. Joshua stays by the Tabernacle so we can have Moses' help. We'll soon be ready to travel onward.

I'm uneasy about the experience we're facing. "Moses," I say, "It seems to me we are just one big nation of complainers! There was lots of anger and arguing when we changed positions just a few days before Passover. How can many thousands of travelers make a longer trip without griping and grumbling—or rebelling?"

"How it must grieve God!" Moses says, sadly. "I hope all of the Israelites will do better, when they realize they will be getting closer to the Promised Land, with each step they take."

Then he tells me how God had instructed him about the whole project, so that it is well organized. As soon as the priests blow the trumpet's signal for the journey to begin, Judah's troops are to lead the way, joined by the tribes of Issachar and Zebulun.

They will be strong protectors for the Tabernacle, which will be taken down under the priests' supervision and transported by the Gershonite and Merarite divisions of Levites. With wagons and oxen, they will follow closely behind the leading eastern tribes.

I, ZIPPORAH

"The troops of Reuben, Simeon, and Gad will march next," Moses explains. "The Kohathites will follow, bearing the sacred objects, and while they are on their way, the Gershonites and Merarites will already be setting up the Tabernacle at the new location. When the Kohathites arrive with the precious furniture and all the utensils, the priests will oversee placing every item," Moses says, confidently.

Each tribe will march according to the order given by the Lord to Moses. Troops of Ephraim, Manasseh, and Benjamin are next in the march, each tribe carrying its own banner, as do all the other tribes. Dan's troops go last. They serve as the rear guard for all the tribal camps, with Asher and Naphtali joining in the rear guard group, filling a vital need for our protection.

My head is swimming with names and positions, as Moses gives me the facts—facts I had asked for but far more than I expected.

Again I realize we have a wonderful God Who cares about the details of life. And I want to thank Him!

As we start on our way, Jochabed insists on walking. She is old, but she is so eager to get to the Promised Land that her feet keep moving—until I see she is too tired to continue. I help her onto the donkey. I thought Eliezer would ride with his grandma, but he slides off, instead, and toddles along beside me, until he stumbles in the dust too many times. Then I make a bit of space for him in the cart. Soon he is asleep.

"Mo-mo, may I walk with you today?" Gershom had asked earlier, as we were busy packing. And so, following the troops which lead the march, Moses and Gershom join the Kohathites, marching together in the growing sunshine.

I'm a wee bit envious. I want to be with my Moses!

After a few hours Gershom tires and chooses instead to ride with Eliezer on our faithful donkey. Jochabed rides in the cart.

My many years of herding sheep have given my legs strength to keep going. It doesn't take long for me to catch up with Moses. My heart sings, as we walk together in the vast crowd of Israelites.

After a small noon meal, Moses picks up Eliezer to straddle across his shoulders. Eliezer's smile is from ear to ear. I suspect Moses' grin is just as broad, hidden by his whiskers. Eliezer is high above the dust now, dust stirred up by hundreds and thousands of marching feet. Jochabed and I are both coughing.

The cloud of God's Presence leads us on, until the sun begins to lower in the sky. Then our journey halts, and we see the Lord's Tabernacle quickly being set up.

Moses had told me that each worker was assigned *by name* to his distinct part in the Tabernacle's erection. Each socket, each cord, each bar, each curtain—each piece—has its care-taker.

Now I see the marvelously organized plan in action. The Tabernacle's rising seems almost like a miracle. Everything is in place when the Kohathites arrive with the sacred furniture.

I know I dare not see the Ark of the Covenant go into the Most Holy Place. Then the curtain-veil will be hung on its posts. From our shelter, I see the altar of incense and the other sacred pieces, being carried to the priests, to put into their proper settings within the Holy Place. Soon the lamps will be lit.

East of the Tabernacle door the bronze altar is being readied for the evening offering and the bronze laver filled with water so the priests may wash.

The glorious cloud hovers wide above every campsite, becoming fiery as darkness deepens. We're weary from the journey, but this is a time for great rejoicing! We are well on our way to the Promised Land! Instead of sleeping early tonight, travelers gaily chat together.

God, the Creator

After our sons are asleep, Moses and I sit and talk, as the embers of our fire slowly become ashes.

"I feel well-protected here, with God's cloud hovering over us like a mother hen spreading her wings over her chicks," I say to the dear man at my side. "And with the cloud glowing with fire, surely any enemy nations will fear."

I'm contented, but I realize *I miss seeing the stars!*

"Moses," I ask, "Do you think it's true that stars are angels holding candles? And if it's true, who puts them there every night?"

"Is that what you were told when you were a child ?" Moses asks me.

"Basemath said so, but I don't know if she really knew, or was just guessing. What do you think? Did your ancestors teach Israelites about stars?"

The last ember has burnt out. Moses and I sit alone by our tent. I love times like this when just the two of us can share thoughts.

"I don't know what stars are made of," Moses says, "but I know Who made them and put them there."

"You know who made them? Who?" I'm like a child again, eager to learn about many things which are mysteries to me yet.

"Before there was anything—no earth, no sky, no moon nor stars—our great God, the One Who sees and hears and speaks, was already God. He created everything that exists."

"You mean He made the stars? They are so beautiful! How thoughtful of God to have made such beauty for people to enjoy!"

Moses agrees. "Yes, our God is truly wonderful!"

"What about animals and people? Did everything we can see begin with Him?"

"Everything!" Moses answers. "Even the sand on which we're sitting. He deserves to be loved and worshiped, with all our hearts and souls and minds and strength."

"Oh, Moses!" I say. "I never heard, before, about the Creator God. I feel so stupid! Does everyone else know that trees and flowers and water and earth and animals and even people were made by Someone and couldn't have been put here by accident? Am I alone in my ignorance?"

Moses says I'm not. "Everyone can see what God has made, and they can know the Creator God if they want to," he says. "But many people have chosen not to honor God and acknowledge His glory. They have thought up their own ideas about how the things of this world came to be, and then they have made their own gods to agree with their theories."

Moses sighs deeply, and adds, "God wants the very best for the people He has made. He wants them to obey Him and live righteously, but too often they want their own ways instead, and so they rebel against Him."

"How dreadful!" I exclaim. "All the Israelites surely know about the Creator, and still they often resist what they know is right! How God must grieve!"

We sit quietly for several minutes. I hear Eliezer mumble something in his sleep, and I say goodnight to this precious man, and go to my bed.

Thoughts I never dreamed I might think rumble through my head as I fall asleep.

Intermission

I don't feel ready to move after only a too-short sleep, but the wondrous cloud lifts, the silver trumpets blow, and we must resume our journey in this wilderness of Paran. We'll travel slowly, giving the livestock plenty of time to enjoy the lush pastures.

While we gather manna this morning, I hear women moaning about the rigors of this trip. Today's complaints are more than yesterday's, and more women join the morning grumbler's chorus. I hear Moses' name mentioned often—and not in a complimentary way. (Talk gets quieter when they spy me, but still I hear a little of it whispered in my direction.)

As we amble along now, I try to introduce more interesting topics for discussion than fault-finding. I look for a few low-growing flowers hiding under the grass. Their muted colors are easily missed until I point them out. Then women brighten—temporarily.

Surely all women like to talk about their children. Asking timely questions turns the gabble toward the boys and girls among us. I hear much bragging about the intelligence of certain little sons or the beauty of certain daughters. To my ears the boasting is ridiculous. But it beats whining!

Perhaps listening to the other women will help me learn how to be a better mother. Recently my big struggle is trying to understand my little son's babble. Gershom seems to figure it out, somehow. To me, it's only gibberish.

This son of Moses is full of questions about every new thing. How do I know it's a question? Eliezer raises his left eyebrow, just like his grandfather Jeh-Jeh did! "What's this?" says the eyebrow, and

"What is that?" And I do my best to explain. Just now he comes to me greatly excited about something. "Tuh-tuh," he says, and repeats, "Tuh-tuh! Tuh-tuh! TUH-TUH! **TUH-TUH!**"

I don't understand. I simply stand here puzzled.

Suddenly, he crouches down. He tucks his knees under his belly and his feet under his backside. His arms huddle under hunched shoulders, with his head bowed low on the ground.

"Eliezer!" I exclaim. "You look like a turtle!"

Instantly he unfolds. "Tuh-tuh! Tuh-tuh, Mommy!" he chirps happily. He grabs my hand and pulls me with eagerness—to see a desert turtle he has found!

He claps in glee. I clap with him! I see hope for understanding him. I need to observe him in action, and then listen—with much patience—to speech that is unintelligible to my untrained ears, but must indeed be heard with my heart.

After our night's meal—a young kid boiled with manna and desert vegetation—Moses and I have a bit of time together as the embers burn out. I tell him about the women's grumble-chorus of the morning. Rather gloomily he tells me he has been hearing increasing complaints as he travels with this multitude.

I wish I hadn't told him about the women and their grumbling. He doesn't need my help to feel depressed. How can I cheer him tonight?

Suddenly I remember Eliezer and the turtle episode. I tell Moses the whole story, even trying to act it out, although I can't possibly do it as well as our little son did. Moses throws back his head and laughs and laughs, until tears run down his cheeks.

"How I wish I could have seen him!" he says, and laughs some more.

The last embers have died. Moses hugs me and goes chuckling to his tent in front of the Tabernacle entrance. I lie awake a long while.

God Deals with Complainers

Tomorrow is Sabbath, and we shall rest from traveling—and hearing tiresome murmurs and laments, which, on this hot afternoon, are far worse than before. Do these whiners think God cannot hear what they're saying? Perhaps they suppose He enjoys the ingratitude of travelers—travelers to the Promised Land!

Sudden fire begins in the outskirts of the camps. Screaming with fear and pain, and with clothing in flames, the people cry out to Moses. Moses prays, and the fire is quenched.

Moses names the place Taberah (burning). He tells them the fire of the Lord had burned there because God was greatly displeased by all their complaining.

There are many requests for extra olive oil to soothe surface-burned bodies, and there are many mourners for those who didn't survive. I hear no grumbling now.

Israelites seem to be slow learners—even with God as the teacher. Days ago, fire had broken out because God was angry with the complainers. Today it seems they haven't learned their lesson.

During days of our long trek through hills and valleys, cattle and sheep have grazed their fill and are contented. God's chosen people might have learned from the livestock to be satisfied with what God freely gives us. But learn we don't.

This evening some who came with us from Egypt begin craving other food than manna. They stir up the Israelites to believe they are being deprived. Forgetting their years of cruel slavery, Israelites lust for foods they had eaten in Egypt: leeks, onions, garlic, cucumbers, melons, fish.

"We want meat to eat!" they begin to yell. "We remember the good food we had in Egypt, but we're completely shriveled up now, because there's nothing for us to eat except this *manna*!"

Our little family can't enjoy the evening meal because of the wailing we hear all around us. Standing at the door of their tents, families weep and sob, and cry aloud, "We're tired of this *manna*. We want *meat*!"

God's anger is greatly aroused, and Moses is very troubled. I don't recall ever seeing him this distressed before. He leaves his food uneaten and goes to the Tabernacle where he and the Lord have often talked together.

I hold back tears and try to be cheerful so that Gershom and Eliezer can eat in peace. After they finish their meal, I make up a silly little game, and the three of us play until it's time for them to go to bed.

Then I dare to weep. I try to pray to the God Who hears. I ask Him to comfort His anguished servant, who speaks with Him tonight in the Tabernacle.

The boys are asleep when Moses finally comes back to our tent. We sit together in the darkness and talk softly.

He tells me how he had cried out to God, the One Who dwells between the cherubim, whose wings hover over the Mercy-Seat on the Ark of the Covenant.

I just listen, stroke his hand with my fingers, and let the tears roll.

Moses tells me, with sobs, that he had complained to God, "Have mercy on me! What did I do to deserve having to bear the burden for all these people? Did I give birth to them? Must I carry them in my arms like a nursing mother? You want me to guide them to the land You promised their ancestors, but they rebel each step of the way! They keep whimpering to me to give them meat. I can't do everything they want. The burden of all these people is too heavy!"

He stops, wipes his eyes and nose, sniffs, and goes on. "I told God that if this is the way He's going to treat me, I'd rather He'd just let me die right now!"

"Oh, Moses!" I whisper. "I don't want you to die!"

"I was angry!" Moses says. "Then the Lord spoke to me, with words of love. I didn't deserve His kindness, his mercy. But He had compassion for me!" He stops speaking, to cough and wipe his eyes.

My dear man goes on, "He told me to gather together, before Him, seventy men who are known to be elders and leaders. They are to come to the Tabernacle and stand with me. He said He will come and talk with me there."

Moses clears his throat and continues. "Then clearly He spoke to me, 'I will lift some of the Spirit which is on you, and I will put the Spirit on them as well. They will help you in the care of the Israelites so that you will not have to bear the burden alone.'"

"Oh, Moses!" I exclaim. "How good is your God!"

"*Our* God," Moses corrects me, with a feeble smile. "He is your God now, is He not? But there's more I need to tell you."

"I'll listen," I promise.

"God told me an astounding thing to say to the people," Moses says. "They are to purify themselves, because the next day they will have meat. God said He heard all their whining about better food back in Egypt. They wanted plenty of meat instead of manna. And so God will give them meat, and they must eat it—for an entire month until they gag and vomit!"

"What!" I exclaim. "There are at least 600,000 men here, plus many women and children. How can they have enough meat for an entire month, even if they kill all the livestock?" I am incredulous. Is this just Moses' imagination?

"I said almost the same thing to God. I argued that what He said was impossible," says Moses, bowing his head low. "I doubted

God. He is holy. He cannot lie. How could I have doubted His words?"

"Moses!" I say. "You doubted God? But you were with Him for forty days on Mount Sinai, and You saw His glory. You have talked with Him face to face as good friends do. Did you really doubt Him? How can You and He be friends now?"

"Yes, I truly didn't believe what He said tonight. I was so wrong—so unholy! He said to me, 'Have I lost all My power? You will see that I speak truth.'"

God Who hears and knows my heart, I dare not doubt Your words. You will surely accomplish what You promised. Please forgive my unbelieving heart.
And please don't give up Your friendship with Moses!
I whisper my prayer to the Lord, and I know He hears and loves me enough to do what I ask Him. Thank You, great and holy God.

The cloud rests over the Tabernacle today, and we also rest.

But only for a little while!
The wind begins to blow—hard. The Lord makes the wind bring tremendous flocks of quails from the sea. They fly about waist-height all around the camp, for miles in every direction. Those who had hungered for meat go out and catch quails all the rest of the day, and even all night. Still the next day there are quails to gather.

And gather the people do! Each family has piles of quails on the ground. When no more quails fly, the people spread the birds all around the camps to sun-dry. They eat quails. They eat more quails. And they eat more quails.

With meat for which they had cried two days ago, they gorge themselves until they become so ill they begin to vomit.

The Lord's anger blazes against them, and He strikes them with a severe plague. Hundreds die. Moses names the place Kibroth-hattaavah—graves of gluttony.

Fighting Bitterness

For almost a month the cloud has stayed over the Tabernacle, so we remain here. Now the cloud lifts and guides us to Hazeroth. Perhaps we can stay here a few weeks. The vegetation looks plentiful for our livestock—and our families.

Even after there were many deaths from the plague at Kibroth-hattaavah, the people become discontented, and begin again to complain. I should be used to it by now, I suppose, but I'm not.

What happens today is not just the usual griping and whining. This is personal, and my heart is struggling against bitterness.

As I step out into the sunshine this morning, I hear Miriam and Aaron criticizing Moses—because he had married a foreigner! This really hurts! When Moses tries to explain that God Himself had arranged our marriage, they both turn on him.

"Has God spoken only through you? Hasn't He also spoken to us?" they ask scornfully.

Moses doesn't argue. But the Lord hears the whole thing. He calls Moses with Aaron and Miriam and tells them to go to the Tabernacle, where He descends in the pillar of cloud at the entrance.

I am not close enough to hear what happens next, but Moses tells me later. He says God calls Miriam and Aaron to step forward, and speaks very sternly to them. He tells them that if there were prophets among us, He would speak to them in dreams or in visions, but that He speaks *clearly* to Moses.

Humbly, Moses bows his head, and tells me, "God said He trusts me. He told the two of them that He speaks to me face to face—and that I see Him as He is."

The Lord was very angry with them for daring to criticize him, Moses says. God didn't talk more with them. Instead, the cloud lifted from above the Tabernacle, and, he tells me, with sadness in his voice, that there stood Miriam with her skin *white with leprosy!*

Aaron cries out to Moses then, and admits they have sinned foolishly. Moses turns to the Lord and pleads for Miriam's healing. But God says, "If her father had just spit in her face, she would be unclean and remain outside the camp for seven days. So put her outside for seven days. Then she'll be allowed back."

We'll remain in Hazeroth and not travel until Miriam is back with us. Then we will go farther north, nearer to the Promised Land. We'll soon be there!

About the bitterness in my heart—yes, it is painful to know what they think about me. God Who hears, God Who knows everything, please teach me how to deal with inner pain without becoming angry or bitter. I know such attitudes will not glorify You. I choose to honor You. I mustn't give in to self-pity.

Today I learn from Eliezer! Three little boys, all older than he, are playing together with him. He keeps telling them something that sounds like "sih-dow". The boys don't understand and begin to laugh at him and mock his words. He knows they are making fun of him. His left eyebrow lifts to ask "why?"

He doesn't cry. He doesn't get angry. He *laughs.* Again he says "sih-dow", plops down on the ground, and pats the ground beside him. They eventually respond to his signal and also plop onto the ground. Suddenly, he puts one foot behind his head. The other boys gape in astonishment. They try to do the same thing, but one by one they fall over. Now they laugh *with* him instead of *at* him. And they are friends.

I want to tell Moses about this—*but I don't intend to act it out!* I do intend to work at teaching my little fellow how to speak clearly. (How to say, "*Sit down!*")

Almost at Canaan

We're at Kadesh, just a short distance from the Promised Land! Moses is eager to go on, but the cloud rests on the Tabernacle, and we wait. This area in the desert is a vast oasis, surrounded by hills. It feels quite safe for us Israelites, even though we know we're in hostile territory.

Several pools and wells are in the wadi where we camp, and there is much grass for grazing—and flowers for gazing. I even discover a few fig trees, which add to our supper.

Burnt offerings are offered each day, some as sin offerings, some for thanksgiving, and some as peace offerings, pleasing the Lord with the aroma. The fire on the altar never goes out—unless, of course, we're on the march, which we hope to begin very soon.

At this place where we're camping, we can see, far in the distance, the green hills of the Promised Land. I ask Moses, "Why don't we just go on?"

Moses says the Lord told him he must first send some men to spy out the land (called Canaan) which God promised to Abraham. One leader from each tribe is to be chosen. He tells me that one of those leaders, from the tribe of Ephraim, is Moses' very special aide, the wise and godly Joshua.

Moses tells the men to go north, through a desert place, and into the hill country. "Very thoroughly, look over all the land and its inhabitants," Moses says, "and bring back complete reports." Are there many trees for building? Are the cities walled, or open like camps? Are the people many or few? Are they strong or weak?

We want to know if the land where we are going is fertile. They should bring back samples of crops growing there. This is the season for harvesting grapes, so they should bring back some grapes, and other fruit, Moses tells the twelve men.

After Moses gives these twelve spies detailed instructions, he sends them out.

We wait. And wait. And wait.

The cloud remains over the Tabernacle each day and glows with fire each night.

Forty days and forty nights pass.

Return of the Spies

As this new morn is breaking, I hear the shout, "Here come the spies!"

Sunrise peeps over the horizon, and I see them trudging east toward the Tabernacle, where they will report to Moses and Aaron. In great excitement thousands of men, and some women, quickly assemble to hear the report, jostling for the best view of the twelve who are coming down the final rise and into the camp.

I can't believe my eyes! I blink again in the early sun. My eyes don't deceive me. I see a huge cluster of grapes so large two men are carrying it on a pole! I slip closer and see they also have samples of wheat and barley, and some figs and pomegranates. The fruit is so plump and beautiful it calls forth loud cheers.

All of us want to hear the report, and finally we quiet down enough to listen. I hear them tell Moses that the land is indeed a bountiful country—a land flowing with milk and honey.

The people cheer boisterously when they hear such good news. They yell, "Let's go! We're ready for the Promised Land!" I'm dancing for joy, and so are many other women. Children, recently awakened, look rather bewildered, but soon they too are caught up in the excitement.

Caleb from the tribe of Judah, one of the spies, joyfully shouts, "Let's go at once and take the land. We can surely conquer it!"

But some begin listening to other spies, fearful ones who cry, "The people there are very strong, and their cities are fortified with high walls. We even saw giants there. They were great and tall! We felt like grasshoppers in their sight. The land will simply devour anyone who goes there. We can't go up against them!"

I can't hear everything that's being said, but I hear enough to guess what will happen next. Even my worst guess wasn't nearly so bad as what's happening now. Almost the whole crowd begins to wail. Their shrieks and screams in furious protest against Moses and Aaron get increasingly raucous.

As morning turns into noon, and then into afternoon, even more men join. By evening it has become a real riot. Many wives are now joining in the melee as darkness overtakes us. Children are very frightened. Their cries are pitiful.

Tonight I do my best to explain to Gershom and Eliezer that God is taking care of us. They are too young to comprehend the reason for the awful racket which echoes from the hills around us. *I'm too young, too!* This is like the sound of war!

How can I sleep? From my tent door I hear what people are yelling. "Oh, why didn't we die in Egypt or even in this wilderness?" they wail. "Does God want to take us to this country so we will be killed in battle and our wives and children captured as plunder? The time has come to return to Egypt! Let's get a new leader and … "

Moses and Aaron have fallen face down on the ground. Joshua and Caleb rip their clothes, and as loud as they can they call to the people, "That land is a wonderful land! If the Lord is pleased with us, He will take us there and keep us and our children safe!" Those two faithful spies plead at the top of their voices, "Don't rebel! Don't be afraid! The people of the land have no gods to protect them, but our powerful God is with us. He will fight for us. Let's go!"

Now, amid the ugly uproar, there are shouts about stoning Joshua and Caleb. I am much afraid. Help us, God!

Suddenly everyone sees the glorious Presence of the Lord over the Tabernacle, and they hear the Lord speaking, though they don't understand the words. Moses will tell them tomorrow what God says.

The rioting crowd slowly breaks up then. At last there is a bit of peace, though whining and grumbling still persist, as they go to their own camp sites. I hope their children somehow sleep tonight.

Moses' Plea

Around midnight, Moses comes and tells me what God has said to him. In dim lamp-light I see his tear-stained face, and when he begins to tell me what the Lord said, the tears come again, and mine flow with them.

"How long will these people treat Me with utter contempt?" God questioned. "Will they still not believe Me even after I've done many miracles for them?"

Moses says he had no answer for God, and God continued with dire words.

"They will not be My people any longer! I will destroy them with a plague. Instead I will make you into a greater and mightier nation than all of them are now!"

I weep with Moses, as he tells me what God had said He would do to the people whom He had called His special treasure. And I weep more when Moses tells me how forcefully he argued with God. He told the Lord, he says, that all the nations would hear about it. They would say God was too weak to bring these people into the land He had promised them, and so He killed them in this desert.

I can scarcely breathe as Moses goes on. He says he reminded God of His unfailing love, forgiving sins and rebellion, but not excusing guilty persons. "Please, God," he had pleaded, "Show again Your marvelous love by pardoning the sins of the people, as You have forgiven them many times since they left Egypt."

How can God keep on forgiving these rebellious sinful Israelites? I think if I were God even for a few days, I'd have gotten rid of all of us! He showed Himself to us over and over in the cloud that hovers over us. Don't we see? Don't we care that He loves us? Or do we want Him to become our *servant* to do whatever we want?

I'm grateful our boys are sound asleep and don't hear all that their father is telling me tonight.

Moses is weeping copiously, and I with him. He is a truly great man, but still he's just a human being. God's love for him is *wonderful*, so wonderful that He listens to his arguments and heeds his pleading. I do not understand God! He is so good!

I bring Moses a cup of water. He drinks it all in two gulps. I bring another cupful. Finally he tells me the tragic rest of the story. We both weep more.

"The Lord told me," Moses says, "that He will do what I asked and pardon the people, and not destroy them, but that none of these rebels shall ever enter that land. They had seen His glorious Presence and the miracles He had done, but they refused to listen to His voice and obey Him."

God had said to Moses, "None of the contemptuous ones will even get an opportunity to see that land. But Caleb was My true servant. He has been loyal and has a righteous attitude different from the others. I will take him into the land he explored, and his descendants will possess their full share."

What will happen to all of the rest of us?

Moses is exhausted and heartsick. But it's almost dawn. Soon he must face the people and give them God's message. He drinks another cup of water and slides onto the tent floor. His weary body rests until the sun begins to rise.

The priests blow the signal from the Tabernacle entrance, and criticizers, and grumblers, and complainers—the rebels—assemble, again loudly protesting. When the cloud hovers low, Moses and Aaron begin to speak.

But the people don't want to listen to what God says. Then …

They die! Those ten spies—the men who gave a bad report and incited rebellion *die before the Lord!*

The people become fearful of *not* listening! Now Moses and Aaron can speak.

They tell the people that God says, "The very things you feared will truly happen to you because you complained against Me. Those of you who are twenty years old and older, all who were included in the registration, will not enter nor possess the land I promised you."

With the exception of Caleb and Joshua, Moses tells them, they will all die in this wilderness. No, their children will not be plunder; they will enter the land and possess it. Before they go in, however, they must wander in the wilderness for *forty years*, one year for each day the spies checked out the land. Their children and grand-children will suffer because of their parents' unbelief in God's eternal love and faithfulness.

Moses and Aaron tell them plainly that the Lord says, "I will do these things to every member of the community who conspired against Me. You will regret what you have done because I will no longer be your friend. I, the Lord, have spoken."

Then the people are filled with great grief. But instead of being with their families to grieve, hundreds of the men get together and plan an assault. Early the next morning, they strap on their weapons and begin to climb.

"Let's go," they say. "It's true we have sinned, but now we're going to go into the Promised Land."

Moses must have been ready to tear his hair! "Why do you now disobey God's orders? He says you must turn around and go back into the wilderness. You dare not do this because the Lord is not with you. You'll be smashed by your enemies, slaughtered because God will abandon you as you have abandoned Him."

Moses tells me all about this later, in this tragic day. The arrogant rebellious ones, defying God, start up to the hills. Moses and the Ark of God's covenant do not leave camp, so they have no protection. Canaanites and Amalekites, who live in those hills, attack them and slaughter those who can't run away. I don't know how many of them die there. The graves are myriad.

Now the people truly grieve. They weep before the Lord, but He doesn't listen.

We'll stay at Kadesh until the Lord leads us away. Then, following His cloud, we must turn back into the terrible desert with stinging scorpions and slithering serpents. And our journey will not be for only a few weeks.

We must wander for forty years!

Forty years!

Memories

Forty long miserable years of wandering! After miles and miles of desert, with sparse and often thorny growth, and some very ugly creatures, I'm thankful to be at last in the Kadesh area again.

Early this morning, I go alone to bathe. There is no breeze, and the clear pool is placid. As I bend to wash, I am startled to see the image of a stranger in the water-mirror, someone with grey-streaked long black hair, falling over slightly wrinkled cheeks. The image gasps when I gasp, and frowns with me in disbelief.

Forty years have exacted a costly toll!

I hug to my heart forty years of memories of God's faithfulness in leading His people, and in *teaching us His ways,* sometimes through very hard lessons.

The Lord wants Israel to be a holy nation and represent Him and His holiness to all the world. Through these past forty years I have grown to know Him better and trust Him with all my soul.

However, I'm left with some memories I would prefer to forget *but cannot.*

His punishments for disobedience are part of His teaching, to purify a people for Himself. Moses had carefully given Israel all God's commandments. None of them are too difficult to obey, by those who truly desire to please the Lord. If anyone should refuse to be completely obedient, thinking a small disobedience may be overlooked, *God will see,* and will deal with that one righteously.

One of the memories I'd like to forget is of vultures circling over a spot far outside the camp. Moses told me, "God saw the heart of a man who, despising His word, insolently went out yesterday, *on the Sabbath*, and gathered sticks for his fire." God told Moses the people should drag the man outside the camp and stone him to death. And so the vultures circled.

The people trembled then. The incident was a powerful reminder of the Lord's commandment to keep the Sabbath day as a holy day of rest!

One memory still gives me nightmares. We hadn't journeyed long into our forty years, before a terrible event. I heard only the beginning of scandalous speech that day, quickly retreated to our tent, and covered my ears to drown out the sounds of evil jealousy.

With great grief, Moses, later, told me some of the horrendous story.

A Levite named Korah, a grandson of Kohath, conspired with Dathan and Abiram, Reubenites, to rise up against Moses and Aaron. Together, they gathered two-hundred-and-fifty of the most well-known representatives of each tribe, and made scathing accusations against the high priest and against Moses.

"You think too much of yourselves," they yelled. "Do you think you are the only holy ones in Israel? All the congregation is holy, and the Lord is with them. Why do you exalt yourselves above all the rest of us?"

Moses fell on his face and cried out to God. Then he said to Korah and his group of conspirators, "Tomorrow we'll find out who is holy and who may come close to the Lord. God Himself will choose!"

I know God has separated all the Levites to work for the Lord in the Tabernacle, and to serve the congregation as God's representatives. Evidently Korah and his clan wanted a higher place, and were envious of Aaron and his position.

Why did they also stir up Dathan and Abiram to quarrel against Aaron and Moses? What could take over men's hearts to cause them to devise such wickedness?

Moses said he told those two-hundred-and-fifty men to take censers, put fire and incense in them, and stand at the Tabernacle door the next morning. They did.

There the glory of the Lord appeared to all Israel.

I remember how brilliantly the sun shone that morning, as I dared to come from our tent to see what was happening. Moses was speaking in a strong voice. He told everyone to get away from the tents of Korah, Dathan, and Abiram, and not to touch anything of theirs lest they die.

"Here's how you'll know who is doing the Lord's work, by His power," Moses shouted. "If these men die in the normal way, then I am not God's messenger to all of you. But if the ground where they're standing opens up and swallows them and everything they own—if they go down alive into the pit and the earth completely covers them—then you will know who has rejected God."

Instantly, the earth split wide open. Korah, Dathan, Abiram, and all they owned went down, with their screaming families, into the earth far below, and the ground closed over them. In abject terror all the others scattered far away.

(Moses told me that fire came out from the Lord, and consumed the two-hundred-and-fifty men who were burning incense, which God had not ordained them to do.)

Sometimes in my sleep, I see the ground open its mouth and swallow those who rebelled. I hear hideous shrieks as they perished, and I see barren ground where once their tents stood. It's one memory I'd like to forget completely.

My memory of what happened the very next day is not a nightmare but a reality. I saw the people gather together, and heard them complain against Moses and Aaron. "You have killed God's people!" they yelled. Suddenly the cloud covered the Tabernacle, and the glory of the Lord appeared. The people were filled with great fear.

God was furiously angry, and spoke of consuming them immediately. Moses told Aaron to take a censer, with fire from the altar, put incense on it, and quickly run into the crowd and make atonement for the people, for God had sent a plague among them! When Aaron stood between the dead and the living, the plague ceased to spread—after almost fifteen thousand people died.

"Why?" I had asked Moses later. "If God loves His people, why does He get angry enough to send death?"

Moses stroked his beard slowly before he answered. "Would you want a God Who isn't hard set against every form of evil? Wouldn't He be an accomplice in injustice, and abuse, and violence, and … ?"

"But Moses," I argued, "God is not human. We have temper tantrums and act like children when our emotions get the best of us. How could God have emotions?"

"Love is an emotion, isn't it?" Moses responded. "The difference is that all His emotions are from His *absolute holiness*. So He must hate evil."

"Oh!" I said. "This is something I must chew well, before I swallow. But I promise to chew on it. Thank you, Moses."

Then I received a nice warm hug from my dear and godly man.

I remember the sad day when dear Mother Jochabed died. I loved her very much. When Miriam died not long after, I didn't feel much grief. I had never been close to her. Mother Jochabed must have been around one-hundred-and-thirty years old. Miriam was one-hundred-and-nine (or ten). Because Miriam was considered a prophetess, all Israel mourned for many days, and travel waited.

One colorful memory, I cherish, and laugh to myself, when I think of the chagrin on the faces of the twelve tribal leaders. Because of the constant complaining against the leadership of Aaron (and always of Moses), God told Moses to get a rod from each tribe's leader. Each man's name was to be written on his own rod. Aaron, of the tribe of Levi, also produced his rod, and wrote his name on it.

All the rods were placed in the Tabernacle, before the Ark. God said that the rod of the man He would choose would show life. And so God would get rid of unceasing complaints—to which the people have seemed absolutely addicted!

The next day Moses went into the Tabernacle, gathered the rods, and took them out. All the people could see for themselves.

Aaron's rod had sprouted, grew buds, produced flowers—and yielded ripe almonds! Each of the other tribal leaders picked up his own rod, with his name clearly written on it, and sort of sneaked away, like a puppy with its tail between its legs.

With passion and sorrow is my memory of what happened at Meribah. Once again the complainers and grumblers were practicing for the next show-down with Moses. There was no water where we camped that day, and the refrain was, "Why did you make us come out of Egypt to bring us to this evil desert place? There's nothing good to eat here, and there's no water to drink. We want water! *We want water!*"

At the Tabernacle the glory of the Lord appeared to Moses and Aaron, and God told Moses, "Take your rod, Moses. You and Aaron are to gather the people together as you stand before that rock." God pointed to the specific crag of which He spoke.

Then God told Moses, "Speak to the rock while they are watching, and water shall come out of the rock for the people and all their animals."

Moses had grown sick and tired of all the angry whining and complaining. He finally became so angry that he lost his focus on the God of glory, and for the *first time* he disobeyed the Lord. He said in a loud voice, "Hear now, you rebels! Must we make water for you to come from this rock?" And instead of *speaking* to the rock, he *struck* it twice with his rod. Rivers of clear refreshing water poured from the rock.

But the Lord spoke to Moses and to Aaron, "Because you didn't believe Me, and didn't honor Me, to show My power and holiness before the people of Israel, you shall not bring these people into the Promised Land. You yourselves may not go!"

Oh, how Moses wept as he told me what he had done!

"Moses," I said, "you've never disobeyed God even one time, and for years you've put up with blame and insults from the people. If God refuses to let you go into the Promised Land—well, it seems like extremely severe punishment for only one disobedience."

"God and I talk face to face as friends," Moses said. "I have insulted my precious Friend by claiming honor for myself (and Aaron). Yes, it was only once, but God has chosen me to help the people know Him and His glory."

Moses sobbed, as he continued, "In fury today I disobeyed, and my action *moved the hearts of the people from God onto me!*"

"Oh, Moses," I said, "surely God doesn't expect you never to do anything wrong."

"God wants all of us to be holy, for He is holy," Moses responded. "He wants us to be people who reflect Him and His glory. If I do something wrong, I can be forgiven. But I dare not presume that God won't care if I dishonor Him—*by taking honor that should be His alone.*"

I think I understand, and I want to please You, Lord, by being holy. But I don't trust myself. How I need Your help!

My memory bag is full—forty-years-of-wandering-full. One memory always on my heart is of the conversation we had, on that night under the stars. Now I know more of my man's heart plus much more of the God He worships.

There are sad memories and glad memories. In forty years surely there would have to be some happy ones. Some of my happy ones are of watching our two boys grow from being playful children into diligent men who honor God.

Eliezer's speech progressed rapidly as I did my best to help him. Now he speaks as eloquently as his father, but with twinkling eyes, and an almost impish grin.

He wasn't yet four years old when Gershom began taking him by the hand to the teaching place. Men of Issachar, some who hadn't rebelled and were still on their way to the Promised Land, felt it urgent to review often the stories of the patriarchs.

Young men like Gershom kept adding to their knowledge of God's dealings with Abraham, Isaac, and Jacob. Eliezer ate it up like honey on the comb. Not only did he digest the learning, asking many questions to be sure he had it right, but also he began teaching younger boys, and some girls, too. I have good memories of watching him in action.

As years passed, and as he and his listeners grew older, he enthralled them with the histories of their forefathers by acting out the various parts of each story.

He was Joseph of the coat-of-many-colors, being despised by his brothers, sold into Egypt, thrown into prison for no offense, elevated to Pharaoh's second-in-command, and greeting his brothers roughly when they came to buy food. And then he became the mean brothers who had sold him, and later bowed to Joseph but didn't know who he was.

Eliezer's growing audiences sat wide-eyed, wondering what would happen now. And suddenly, Eliezer would say, *"Continued next time."*

Gershom watched from the sidelines and was pleased with his little brother, who was not so little anymore.

The two brothers are very unlike one another. Gershom grew tall and stalwart like his father, and his beard grew early. Eliezer's almost black hair is like mine (or like mine used to be, before forty years of wandering turned much of it grey). And he's shorter than Gershom.

These two young Levites work in the treasuries, and likely will continue in that capacity after they reach Canaan. Both of them have chosen to honor the great God of Heaven. They have observed Moses these many years since infancy, and want to be like him, by following the true God.

Their Uncle Aaron, brother of Moses and high priest, died during our wanderings. God told Moses, in advance, what to do when we arrived at Mount Hor. He said, "Aaron shall be gathered to his fathers and not enter the land I have given the children of Israel, because he rebelled, with you, against My word concerning the water at Meribah."

Moses took Aaron and Aaron's son Eleazar to the top of Mount Hor. There, at God's instruction, he stripped Aaron of his garments and put them on Eleazar. Aaron died there.

All the people saw the three go up onto Mount Hor, but when only Moses and Eleazar came down, they realized Aaron had died. I remember how the people wept. Their high priest was dead! The mourning lasted for thirty days.

(I wonder if they ever considered that their own blaming and complaining had been a factor in Aaron's death.)

I shudder when I remember what happened as we turned from Mount Hor, going near the Red Sea, to travel the long way around the land of Edom. Edom, the country founded by Jacob's brother Esau, had refused to let Israel go through their land, and so our journey was extra hard and miserable, as we went through harsh desert instead of through Edom.

The people became very discouraged, and again the grumbling grew loud *against God* as well as against Moses. "Why have you brought us out of Egypt and into this desert place where there's no water or food—no food except this worthless manna which we loath? Did you bring us here to die, we and our children?"

Because the people complained *against God*, He sent serpents, fiery serpents, slithering among the people. Many in Israel died from the fatal venom. Then the people came to Moses and confessed their sin of speaking against God, and against Moses, too. "Pray to the Lord," they begged, "to take away the serpents from us."

God told Moses to make a replica of a fiery serpent, and put it on a pole. "Tell the people that everyone who has been bitten but then looks upon the serpent on the pole—that one shall not die but live," God said.

Moses made a serpent of bronze, and hung it on a pole. As surely as God had said, everyone who was bitten by a serpent and simply *looked* upon the bronze serpent on the pole did not die.

(Sadly, I can imagine someone saying, "Humph! Does Moses think I'm some sort of idiot who would believe God said this? God can talk to me as much as He wants, if He thinks I'm stupid enough to swallow such a ridiculous idea." And then he'll groan, roll over onto his side, and die!)

The sweetest memory from those forty years of wandering brings happy tears for me—and for Moses. We are grandparents!

Three years ago, in an oasis with palm trees and springs of water, Gershom and his wife presented us with their first son, Shubael. Moses held that wee one in his strong arms and lifted him up in praise to the Lord, dedicating him to the great God of all the earth, to be His righteous follower all the days of his life.

At Kadesh, my bag of memories is tucked safely away, and we move on to Canaan!

Moses, a Warrior?

Moses is well over one-hundred-years-old. Is he to be a warrior for Israel, in the battle against the Amorites?

Israel has requested permission from King Sihon to pass through their territory on our way to the Promised Land. Sihon refuses. Instead, he gathers together his troops and comes out against Israel. God gives Israel the victory over Sihon and the Amorites. Israel takes possession of Sihon's land from Arnon, which borders Moab, to Jabbok at the border of Ammon.

There are more battles ahead before we reach the Promised Land.

We turn, and go up by the way to Bashan. Bashan's King Og strikes out, with all his people, to fight against Israel at Edrei. The Lord says then, to Moses, "Don't be afraid of him. I have delivered him into your hand, with all his people and his land. You shall do the same to him as to the Amorites." And so Israel defeats King Og and his sons and all his people. There are no survivors.

Og was the last of the Rephaite giants, says Moses. I'd like to watch Eliezer describe to his listeners what Og's bed looked like. Moses says it was almost as long as the Tabernacle boards are tall and about as wide as Eliezer is tall. It was made of iron. What else could have held him?

We move again, and this time we camp on the plains of Moab, near the river Jordan, and across from a city called Jericho. We hear that Moab is filled with dread and fear of Israel, because we are so many that we seem to cover the face of the earth. Moabites are afraid of the God they do not know.

But Israel is not enough afraid of the God we do know! Our men follow their lusts for Moab's idol-worshiping women. They go with them to their sacrifices, and bow down to their gods.

Of course, God's anger is hot against the perpetrators. He says to Moses, "Take all the leaders of those who bowed to Baal, and hang the offenders—in the heat of the sun." Moses tells the judges of Israel, "Each one of you must kill all his men who worshiped Baal."

There is a plague among Israel's people because of their great sin. Phinehas, grandson of Aaron the priest, turns back God's wrath when he uses a javelin to kill both a Baal-worshiping woman and the man who brought her into his tent and his bed. God stops the terrible plague which has wiped out twenty-four thousand.

God is pleased with Phinehas, because, God says, "He was zealous with My zeal among them. I am making a covenant with him. He will always be My priest and so will his sons after him. He cares rightly for My honor among the people."

The men of each tribe, twenty years and older, who were able to serve in the army, had been numbered in the second year after we left Egypt. Every man was listed by name. (The Levites were not listed because they were set apart to do the Lord's service.) Now, while we're in the flatlands of Moab, Moses and the priest Eleazar call for another counting.

"Counting seems like a waste of time," I say to Moses, "so why does God want Israel's men counted, very precisely, by tribes?"

Besides knowing the number of men who are able to fight in the battles which are ahead of us, Moses says, the size of each tribe is important for the allotment of land after we get over Jordan, and into the Promised Land at last. Tribes with larger numbers will be given more land than smaller tribes.

"What about the tribe of Levi?" I ask. "Why is no one counting them?"

"Levites," Moses says, "will not own any land. They are to receive tithes from all the tribes, and the use of pasture lands near the Tabernacle, besides portions of burnt offerings, as God directs. They will not be neglected."

Among all who were counted in the wilderness of Sinai, no men remain except Caleb and Joshua. Forty years ago, the Lord had said of the rebels who refused to go into the Land, "They shall surely die in the wilderness." Thousands of carcasses scattered over a vast area prove that God means what He says.

Oh, we are close to the Promised Land! I'm excited! I'm eager to cross over and enjoy being there, at long last. Gershom and little Shubael and Eliezer and I—we shall set our feet on the grassy slopes and beside the waters of that beautiful country.

Gershom tells me that God first promised that land to Abraham many years ago,

"How do you know that?" I ask. He reminds me that, when he was just a little boy, he used to go to the teaching place of Issachar's old men. There he had learned about Abraham and the Promised Land.

"Abraham didn't worship the gods of Ur," Gershom explains. "He worshiped the one real God, *our God*. God told him to go to a country he had never seen before, and he obeyed, without even knowing where he was going. The country to which God took him is the country of Canaan."

We'll be there in just a few more days!

"Abraham believed God," Gershom tells me, "and therefore God called him righteous, and gave him many very special promises."

"What promises?" I ask.

Gershom tells me that one of the promises was that Abraham's descendants would inherit the land upon which he walked. "I'm one of his descendants," he says, "and I'll pass on my inheritance to Shubael and any other sons I may have."

"You said there were promises." I say. "More than one?"

"Yes," he answers. "God promised that Abraham would become father of a great nation … "

"That's Israel!" I interrupt, and Gershom finishes, "and that *all nations* on earth will be blessed through him."

"All nations will be blessed through Abraham?" I ask. "How can that possibly happen?" Gershom doesn't have an answer, though we both know that if God promised it, He will provide the way.

But I'm a bit confused. If God promised all this to Abraham, why were the people of Israel slaves in Egypt? Gershom surely has the answer, but he needs to go home now, and eat a hearty meal. Israel may be in battle again tomorrow, and he must be strong. I'll wait to ask him later.

Moses is writing again tonight. I don't know how many quills he has worn out, nor where he can get a few more. Raven feathers don't provide good quills, I know. Maybe we'll catch a goose soon.

Moses writes almost every chance he gets. He says it's very important to write down *in detail* all of God's commandments, and promises, and warnings. He also writes songs sometimes, for the people to sing for God.

Very soon he will be taken away from me. I wish he and I had more time to talk together before he goes, and oh, how I wish he could go across the Jordan with me to the Promised Land! He told me, yesterday, that he had pleaded with the Lord to let him cross over, and see the good land on the other side of Jordan, and the pleasant mountains, and Lebanon with its cedars.

"I said to Him," Moses tells me, "I've scarcely begun to know Your greatness and Your powerful hand. There is no one like You in heaven or earth who is able to do anything like You can do—marvelous works and mighty deeds."

And then, Moses says, he bowed down, and begged, "Please, Lord, let me cross over." But because the Lord had been angry with Aaron and Moses for taking the honor to themselves in front of all the people, and then striking the rock when God had told him to speak to it, God again said, "No! You shall not go. Speak to Me no more about it."

Moses' Final Message

All Israel has been called to hear what may be Moses' last message. He had taught them statutes and judgments, as the Lord had commanded him to do. Now he is reminding them how to act, when they possess the land before them.

He tells them to observe and obey everything God has spoken. "If you obey," Moses says, "all other nations will acknowledge that Israel is a strong and wise nation."

This day is grey and dismal, with clouds coming and going. Perhaps by nightfall we'll have rain again. At least it's not hot. We'll be standing a long while. Heat would be difficult for the people to endure. And Moses has much to say.

"Take heed to yourselves, lest you forget what great things God has done," he warns them. "Teach your children and grandchildren, so they will know and obey. Remember all of the Ten Commandments which God Himself wrote on two tablets of stone."

With great earnestness and fervency, Moses says, "*Do not ever forget* that you heard God's voice at Mount Sinai, but did not see *any form*. Be sure *never* to corrupt yourselves and make *an image or a statue to bow down to it and worship!*"

All the people are aware that the Lord had been angry with Moses because of them. They knew God had sworn that he wouldn't cross Jordan and enter the good land. They stand silently and solemnly as Moses continues.

"The Lord Himself loves you, and is giving you that land as an inheritance. I must die in this land, but you shall enter the land. When I am no longer with you, do not forget the covenant which the Lord made with you. If you act corruptly and do evil in His sight, you will soon utterly perish from the land. The Lord will scatter you among other peoples, and you will serve their gods, gods made of wood or stone."

I see that the people are distressed by Moses' warning. But he isn't finished. He tells them, "Then you will seek the Lord—and you will find Him, if you seek Him with all your hearts and souls. For He is a merciful God. He will not forsake you totally, for He will never forget the covenant He made with your fathers. And *He will remember the land!*"

I can't take my eyes off Moses. He truly loves these people—people who have treated him with disdain many times, and have disappointed him over and over again. Yet his face shows compassion and fatherly love for them. He yearns for them to be wise, and therefore to prosper, in the land where he himself is not allowed to go. How much he reflects God's heart for them!

He pleads with them, "Consider with all your hearts that God, our God, is Lord over all the earth. There is no other God! Love Him with all your heart, and all your soul, and all your strength."

I hear a distant rumble of thunder, as Moses continues, "Remember that you are a holy people, whom He has chosen to be a special treasure above all nations on the earth. You were not great in number, but only a small nation of slaves in Egypt. Because God loved you, He brought you out and redeemed you from bondage."

Moses tells them not to be afraid, even though other nations are greater than they. "Remember what God did to Pharaoh and all Egypt. Remember the great signs and wonders you saw. Remember God's outstretched arm that rescued you from peril. He will continue to do all this for you, if you will only obey Him. Don't ignore how the Lord led you all this way to test you, so He would know your hearts."

(I think it's important that they also know their own hearts!)

He reminds them that the Lord faithfully fed them with manna every day, and that their clothes and shoes did not wear out all those years. He tells them that God is bringing them into a good land, with springs and streams of water flowing from valleys and hills. There will be barley and wheat, grapevines and fig trees, and much olive oil and honey.

The sun breaks through clouds for moments and then hides again. The clouds darken as the day gets longer. Moses seems not to notice the approaching storm.

With urgency he admonishes them, *"Do not forget the Lord!* When you have plenty to eat, when you are prosperous in the land, do not forget Who it is Who gives you more than enough. If you should say in your heart that your own strength and might has given you everything you need, if then you forget the Lord, and begin to follow after and serve other gods, I tell you that *you shall surely perish."*

I sense a collective shudder, but Moses continues. "You will destroy the nations ahead of you, not because of *your righteousness,* but because of *their wickedness*! Guard yourselves against becoming arrogant and thinking that your own power or strength has given you victory. God alone is your source!"

Eliezer notices that his father's voice is becoming husky, and he takes a bowl of water to him. He drinks all of it gladly. Perhaps he will dismiss the people.

Not so! He wipes his beard, clears his throat, and continues talking earnestly.

He warns the people to be without fault before the Lord their God. He insists they must be blameless and never be involved with witchcraft, soothsayers, spiritists, and all other such evils, which God calls *abominations*.

Then he openly names evil sensual deeds done by idol-worshiping men. "Keep your own hearts pure," he pleads.

I remember well the fright of the people at Mount Sinai. Now Moses reminds them of that day. "You asked that you not hear the voice of the Lord or let you see the great fire anymore, for fear you would die." Moses adds, "And the Lord agreed with what you had asked. Now I will tell you what amazing words the Lord spoke then."

Moses long ago passed on to me the words God said to him that day. When he first told me, I didn't consider it deeply, because I knew Moses spoke for God to the people, and surely Moses was enough.

I was a beginner in knowing God then. I hadn't thought far ahead to the time Moses wouldn't be speaking any longer. Certainly I hadn't wanted to think anyone would ever take his place! Now my heart remembers and begins to understand.

Today, it is time to tell the people those amazing words God had spoken, words of great promise, followed by severe warning.

Moses says that God told him, "I, the Lord your God, will raise up for Israel a Prophet like yourself from among your brothers. I will put My words in His mouth, and He shall speak to them everything that I command Him."

A Prophet like Moses? All the people are perplexed, but Moses goes on to give God's warning to the people about that Prophet. "And it shall be that anyone who will not listen or obey My words which He shall speak in My Name shall be guilty."

Thunder rumbles closer now. Rain threatens. The river has already risen. What will happen if we get more rain tonight? How can we cross Jordan?

Now Moses begins to speak about himself, something I've never heard him do, before the people. He says to Israel, "I am one-hundred-and-twenty-years-old today. I cannot lead you longer. Besides, the Lord has said to me, 'You shall not cross this Jordan.' But the Lord Himself shall cross over before you, and Joshua will be your leader. Do not be afraid of the people who now reside in the land. Be strong and courageous, for the Lord your God is the One Who goes with you. He will not forsake you."

Moses calls Joshua and says to him in the sight of all Israel, "You must go with the people to the Land which God swore to their fathers to give them. You are the one who shall cause them to inherit it, because the Lord is the One Who goes before you. Do not fear nor be dismayed. God will not leave you."

The sun sinks behind thunderclouds as Moses blesses the people. Everyone goes to his own place, thinking seriously of all Moses has said. (Or at least I hope they are thinking seriously.)

It's been a long day—surely a day in which to consider well what has been spoken by God through Moses, while crescendoing thunder punctuates God's commands and warnings and promises.

"Moses," I say, as he starts toward his tent by the Tabernacle, "Why not join me to eat something? You'll surely have time to write later."

He looks weary as he nods in response. We walk together to my lonely tent. Rain begins splattering as soon as we lift the tent flap. By nightfall it's coming down in torrents.

Moses will not write more tonight. Instead, together we talk long with our glorious God. 'Tis a night I will never forget.

It's no longer raining this morning. When I look toward the Jordan River, I see the water is high and looks muddy. We are to cross the Jordan into the Promised Land. How can that happen?

But crossing the Jordan isn't my first concern this morning. Moses tells me, soberly, that the Lord said to him, "The day is fast approaching when you must die. So call Joshua and present yourselves in the Tabernacle of meeting. I will inaugurate him there to lead My people."

Moses says the two men met in the Tabernacle before the Lord, Who appeared in a pillar of cloud and stood above the door of the Tabernacle. There God Himself commissioned Joshua to be Israel's leader.

The Lord told Joshua that he must keep reminding them of God's commands in their new land. To him God said, "Be strong and of good courage. Bring the children of Israel into the land I am giving them. I will be with you!"

From where we camp, we can see the Jordan River has risen almost to its banks. Is God going to split the Jordan like the Red Sea so the people can cross into Canaan? I am sure that nothing is impossible for God. There is none like Him!

The Last Journey

Moses has finished writing the words of God's law and promises in a book. He commands the Levites who carry the Ark of the Covenant to put the book beside the Ark, as a witness. God's words are to be read, often, to the people.

Also he has written a special song for the people to learn and sing as a reminder and a witness. My favorite part of the song is about eagles. I don't have the whole song memorized yet, but I remember this: "As an eagle stirs up its nest, Hovers over its young, Spreading out its wings, Taking them up, Carrying them on its wings, So the Lord alone led him (Israel), And there was no foreign god with Him."

Moses comes with Joshua and gives all the words of this song to the people. He reminds them once more that they must obey the Lord, and that by keeping God's words, and teaching them to their children, they will prolong their lives in the good land the Lord is giving them.

This very same day the Lord speaks to Moses, saying, "Climb this mountain of the Abarim in Moab across from Jericho. Go to Mount Nebo at the top of Pisgah, and look to the north and east and south and west. There you shall view the land of Canaan which I am giving to Israel for a permanent possession."

Moses is still as strong as a young man. Even his eyes are not dim. But today he will die. He goes to Gershom and to Eliezer, blesses each of them, and kisses each cheek.

Then he and I walk together to the foot of the Abarim range. There we part. I watch as he climbs, vigorously, higher and higher.

Is it only my imagination that the glow of God surrounds him?

Now mountain crags prevent my sight, but I know he will keep climbing until he reaches Mount Nebo, the highest peak. He will have an expansive view of the Promised Land, and then he will die. God will bury him there.

For thirty days Israel will mourn.

I shall miss him, but I shall rejoice. For he is face to face with the Lord of glory, his God—and *my* God.

The End

Author's note

Resources for episodes in this book were from the first five books of the Old Testament, Genesis, Exodus, Leviticus, Numbers, Deuteronomy. (Minor reference: 1 Chronicles 26:23-24.)

About the Author

Maurine Speer Georgiades grew up on a farm on the flatlands of Kansas. By God's design, she transferred to California early in marriage, and for more than sixty years, has resided in the scenic mountain foothills northeast of mega Los Angeles. There she and her husband founded FOIL, an outreach to international students, providing friendship, parties, camps, home-stays, and sightseeing trips.

Maurine is Bible teacher, landscape artist, prankster, writer of numerous articles, and author of four books, of which this is the fourth. Previous books are SHADOW SONG *From Despair to Joy: a Pilgrimage with AIDS*; STITCHES OF GRACE *in the Quilt of My Life*; and FOR LOVE OF ELZY *pioneer life on the prairie: a journal*.

CPSIA information can be obtained
at www.ICGtesting.com
Printed in the USA
FSHW02n1508180618
49304FS